RACE *in* AMERICA

Christians Respond to the Crisis

DAVID MAXWELL *and*
LAURA M. CHEIFETZ, *Editors*

Contributors

Mary Gene Boteler
Laura M. Cheifetz
David Esterline
Jennifer Harvey
Kimberly Jackson
David Maxwell

Otis Moss III
Debra J. Mumford
Tuhina Verma Rasche
Amaury Tañón-Santos
Jessica Vazquez Torres
DeBorah Gilbert White
Frank Yamada

WJK WESTMINSTER
JOHN KNOX PRESS
LOUISVILLE · KENTUCKY

© 2021 Westminster John Knox Press

Revised and expanded edition of a previously published book edited by David Maxwell titled *Race in a Post-Obama America: The Church Responds* (Louisville, KY: Westminster John Knox Press, 2016).

Published by Westminster John Knox Press
Louisville, Kentucky

21 22 23 24 25 26 27 28 29 30—10 9 8 7 6 5 4 3 2 1

Book design by Drew Stevens
Cover design by designpointinc.com
Cover photo: Thomas de Luze / unsplash.com

Library of Congress Cataloging-in-Publication Data is on file at the Library of Congress, Washington, DC.

ISBN-13: 978-0-664-26720-9

CONTENTS

FOREWORD

"How do I live free in this black body?"
—Ta-Nehisi Coates, from *Between the World and Me*

Many pundits hailed the election of Barack Obama as president as the end of all things constructed and construed by race. Over and over I heard men and women who live in gated and cul-de-sac communities trumpet a tale I failed to see. *Postracial* was the term that carried on the airwaves and in the Twitterverse: America had finally realized its noble creed of equality under the law and under God.

Yet as I listened I shook my head, wondering, *What universe do they occupy?* I listened to these words from the South Side of Chicago, where hope and tragedy dance daily for all children who are kissed by nature's sun. The promise of America has not cast its shadow or gazed upon the children who still hold the scars of forced exile and importation to this nation. I do not deny the triumphs, the moments of celebration and progress in our imperfect yet sturdy democracy. But this socially constructed ideology called race remains the original sin of our nation. Our institutions carry the residue and scent of race.

America doesn't see this.

To Ta-Nehisi Coates, impassioned chronicler of the open secret that America struggles to acknowledge, racialized thought and imagined supremacy are the myth and doctrine undergirding our democracy.

As he argues in his book *Between the World and Me*, the nation takes race as a defined and unchangeable reality, like a "feature of the natural world," and therefore feels absolved from doing much about it. He writes,

> Racism—the need to ascribe bone-deep features to people and then humiliate, reduce, and destroy them—inevitably follows from this inalterable condition. In this way, racism is rendered as the innocent daughter of Mother Nature, and one is left to deplore the Middle Passage or the Trail of Tears the way one deplores an earthquake, a tornado, or any other phenomenon that can be cast as beyond the handiwork of men.[1]

In this climate, our common explanations for the persistent disparities that are found in education, criminal justice, housing, and wealth fall into two camps. One argument looks at racial disparities through the lens of poverty, economic policy, and wealth creation and comes to the conclusion that these factors doom the poor, especially poor people of color. The other argument is made through the lens of cultural deficiency, claiming that people of color need to be injected with the wider Protestant work ethic and values of responsibility to close the sociological and material gap.

Sadly, both camps fail to confront the unspoken American belief that Coates names in his writing: being Black and human is considered an oxymoron in much of society.

Blackness is viewed as a deficiency to be expelled from one's psyche or reformed in order to be palatable to the majority culture. More than a century ago, W. E. B. Du Bois spoke of this duality of the African soul that must try to heal in the face of a forced sociological schizophrenia, that "sense of always looking at one's self through the eyes of others, of measuring one's soul by the tape of a world that looks on in amused contempt and pity."[2]

Racism is not expunged by the elimination of Blackness. Racism is not exorcised from the American lexicon through a doctrine of moral deficiency. It is eradicated by Christians only when we reject these myths and come to grips with the beauty of Africanness and dare to live out a new Christianity that is not beholden to European views. We fight these myths by admitting they exist. We fight them by facing the biblical mandate about what the Lord requires: to act justly and to love mercy and to walk with deep humility before God.

As you read through the pages of this book, my prayer is that each chapter will challenge, disturb, and ultimately inspire. America is in need of antiracism activists, preachers, and thinkers who are not people of color. America desires voices with a moral center that dare speak truth to power and walk humbly with our God. These yet-to-be United States wait patiently for your voice, song, poem, essay, sermon, and action to join the cadre of women and men who seek to dismantle and repent from this original sin called racism.

Otis Moss III

PREFACE

The United States and the US church face a reckoning, with some congregations wholly dedicated to Black Lives Matter and providing sanctuary to immigrants at risk of deportation, and others overwhelmingly supporting the election (not once, but twice) to the office of the president a man whose company discriminated against Black people in housing, who called for the death penalty to be used against teenagers wrongly convicted of murder, who announced his candidacy by calling Mexicans murderers and rapists, and who enacted boldly racialized discriminatory policies while declining to condemn white supremacist violence.

This book began to come together in Chicago in the fall of 2008 during a conversation with a diverse group of faculty and staff from McCormick Theological Seminary and local pastors, before the election of President Obama. The group identified a number of topics dealing with racism that churches might discuss. Those initial studies were published online at *The Thoughtful Christian* and were very popular. We took some of those studies, updated them, and added chapters, taking into account the rapidly changing landscape of race relations in the United States. This book was first published toward the end of the presidency of Barack Obama, the first Black president of the United States, when it became clear that racism had not been vanquished.

The nation found itself reeling in a backlash during the Trump administration, exhausted and divided. We realized that the book was in need of a revision to reflect the unfolding and yet timeless white supremacy present in the United States and the U.S. church. Chapters were consolidated and revised, and new chapters were added.

We suggest that you read the entire book; however, feel free to jump to any chapter you like. The book may be read alone, but we hope you will read it with a group of people who want to learn more about racial justice and how to take action. Many more Christians are aware of the scope and scale of white supremacy in the United States and how deeply it is a part of our own institutions, theology, and culture. Whether this is a new perspective for you or an expansion of your existing commitments and understanding, we hope this book will invite discussion and play a role in equipping you and other Christians for the long, difficult work of confession of the sins of white supremacy and repair of the great damage done in U.S. society in the name of white supremacy. May this work be grounded in the deep joy and knowledge that all of us are beloved.

INTRODUCTION

On August 9, 2014, my ministry came full circle in the
death of Michael Brown.

I was raised in Mississippi, a young girl during the first
civil rights movement. When Dr. King walked from Mem-
phis to Jackson down highway 51 to complete the march
started by James Meredith, he walked through our place,
alongside our cotton fields. When our schools were deseg-
regated, I saw children beaten — and I didn't nearly see the
worst of it. Southern pastors who preached too much about
"the situation" were asked to leave. Sympathetic, protesting Northerners who were asked to leave got in their cars
and left. Southerners first had to go by the house and collect their family and belongings.

One Southerner who was asked to leave his pulpit in
Starkville, Mississippi, was Bob Walkup. Years later, as a
young minister, I sat in his living room in Auburn, Alabama,
and heard him tell his riveting story. When he came to the
end, I responded, "Oh, Bob, I don't know what I would do

if I were ever asked to leave a church." He looked at me with kind eyes and said in his gravely voice, "Mary Gene, there are a lot of churches, but you only have one soul. Don't lose it." His words have been a constant source of encouragement to me in my ministry—and I have repeated them hundreds of times.

In some ways, my involvement in the situation around Michael Brown's death was a working out of the demons that plagued me from those earlier experiences. In fact, I have come to believe that God placed me in St. Louis at this particular moment in history, gave me time to develop deep relationships that allowed me to preach God's unrelenting word when the events unfolded in Ferguson. And let's be clear: Ferguson is just a code word for the systemic racism embedded in our institutions and the white privilege that is so ubiquitous that the privileged hardly notice it.

Michael Brown was a young high school graduate who was heading to college. He was raised by his mom, who did everything right. She worked at a well-known St. Louis grocery store chain, along with one of our church's bright graduate students. Michael had a father and a stepfather who loved him. He was no saint, but if the right to live was reserved for saints alone, every pew in America would be empty. As a pastor, I am privy to the white children who struggle with drugs, shoplift in the local stores—and have all their youthful indiscretions buried by sharp lawyers. Michael was not unlike many of the children the church has confirmed and patiently loved into adulthood—only he didn't have the protection that comes with whiteness.

Michael was a Black man in a world that does not value Black lives. There was nothing unique about the death of an unarmed Black teenager at the hands of an overzealous police officer. It happens all the time. What made his situation untenable for the community was the fact that he lay on the ground for over three hours. His mother could not hold him. There was no real attempt to save his life. He lay on the street in front of the community—including children to whom he was like a big brother—and he died.

The reaction of the community was immediate. White clergy sensed that we had to take our cue from the Black community. "What do you want us to do?" we asked. One of the problems is that clergy had not previously built relationships that would allow us to respond quickly in such a volatile environment. That left us in the difficult position of building those relationships while responding to this tragedy. It was messy, and the news media took every advantage of that messiness.

The traditional leaders in the Black community just assumed that they, by default, would direct the response. But quickly it became clear that there was, forming from the grass roots, a group of young leaders who didn't require approval or wait for the direction of their elders or the church. In fact, they viewed the complacency of the older leaders, preachers, and politicians as a mitigating factor in the death of so many young Black men. For too long, they felt the church had suggested that the victims were responsible for their own victimization—pull up your pants, change your diction, and engage in the politics of respectability. What is being called the second civil rights movement is solely the responsibility of these young, brilliant leaders whose desire for freedom absolutely trumps their fear.

The first four months were extremely challenging. Every night there were meetings. Every night there were protests. A small group of clergy from various traditions was trying to follow the live streaming and be present when needed. Generally there was a call for support every night. It was exhausting. We had scores of people coming from out of town for the big events, and they all needed hospitality. Many organizations were trying to provide leadership, and no one was clear about the lane in which they needed to travel. There were those looking to serve, and there were those looking for fifteen minutes of fame. Again, it was messy. Out of that came some remarkable coalitions that continue to meet weekly; one involves sixty or more organizations working together to change the system.

We slept little. On the streets until midnight, we were up and in the office or hospital in the morning. One night while protesting in Ferguson, the group was called to Shaw, another area where another young Black teenager had been killed. When we arrived, the police tape was still up and the investigators were doing their work. Someone pulled me aside to meet the boy's mother. She could only cry and say, "What did I do wrong?" I went to the morgue at 2 a.m. with his father. They would only let him see his son's face, and he left wondering, "Why won't they let me see his body? How are they planning to manipulate the evidence?" I have seen too much not to be skeptical. I have come to understand that trust in the system is another benefit of our whiteness.

I was fortunate to serve a congregation that understood my place to be both in the pulpit and in the street—or, at least, a large majority did.[1] At times it was a balancing act. I had one elder resign from session and the church on Facebook. We exchanged some emails, and by the next morning he wrote, "I would like to stay, if you will have me." I welcomed him with open arms, of course.

The turning point in the movement was the night of the nonindictment. We had known for months that Officer Darren Wilson would not be held accountable. For four months, churches and community groups had been planning for the day. We attempted to work with government and law enforcement officials to develop a plan that would allow people to express their pain, allow the protestors to exercise their First Amendment rights, keep the community safe—and, most of all, value people above property. I have nothing but the harshest criticism for Robert P. McCulloch, the prosecutor, who had no desire to work with the community and, instead, developed a plan that would ensure the worst possible outcome.

On the evening of November 24, 2014, after the non-indictment, our church gathered at 6 p.m. for worship. Following the service, my daughter and I traveled to Ferguson. Even though the crowd knew what was coming, we were holding on to a small ray of hope that justice would be served. When the decision was announced at 9 p.m., it was as if the very life had been sucked from people. There was wailing and crying and the breaking of glass. But then the familiar drumming started and the chanting began—and it was peaceful and cohesive. Suddenly, in the distance, we saw tear gas floating through the air, heading in our direction. We heard gunshots. My daughter and I held hands and tried to run away from the tear gas; we were not entirely successful. As we ran, we stopped to care for some of the people who were the most severely affected. With the help of a stranger, who turned out to be a clergywoman I had not previously met, we headed for our car but were trapped by a police car that was in flames. It had suspiciously been left unattended on the street.

After that night the protests continued, but many of us began moving away from the nightly gatherings and concentrating our work on faith-based organizing. The continuing protests are important, and I have nothing but admiration for those who see that as their role. A wonderful group of interfaith clergywomen began to study together and work for change. We had a number of women's marches. We called ourselves the Wailing Women, after Rachel: "weeping for her children; she refused to be consoled because they are no more" (Matt. 2:18). At one of these marches, I stood near a woman with a picture of her son at various stages in his life, from childhood to graduation. His name was Jeremy. I turned to her and said, "Tell me about Jeremy." And the tears began to pour down her face as she spoke, in great pain, of her beloved son. It was heartbreaking. The community has been filled with opportunities for sacred conversation. And change is coming . . . one *resignation* (the word the establishment uses for "firing") of an official following another. We simply cannot let the movement stall this time.

For eight months, protestors chanted, "The whole damn system is guilty as hell," in a community in which most of the citizens thought the protestors were wrong. But the Department of Justice report is vindication, if not satisfaction. It clearly points out that crimes were committed, Blacks were targeted, lies were told, and that the system is broken beyond a simple mending. What it does not do is hold anyone accountable. And that creates further pain and distrust.

Finally, Ferguson is every community. It is not the worst—not by a long shot. In fact, one could stand in Ferguson and spit in any direction and hit a municipality that is every bit as corrupt and racist. Every state, every city, every community. When we think that our community is different, we "deceive ourselves, and the truth is not in us" (1 John 1:8). There is not a person in the United States who does not live in Ferguson. Our response as people of faith is to decide what our baptism calls us to do about it.

This book is for Christians—especially white Christians living in the United States—to read, discuss with others, and initiate or continue a plan of action to confront racism. Some chapters are informative and offer reflection. Others suggest an array of actions you and your faith community might take. I urge you to take the time to read this book, to pray, to consider what plans of action you might take, to discuss with others, and then to start or continue confronting racism in your church, community, and nation.

Mary Gene Boteler

PART I

RACISM DEFINED
AND RECOUNTED

CHAPTER 1

DEFINING TERMS

Much has been accomplished through civil rights legislation that has paved the way legally for racial equality. Nevertheless, racist attitudes and practices still exist. On the one hand, the election of the first Black president and the first Latina appointment to the Supreme Court offer hope for continued progress toward the elimination of racism. On the other hand, the Supreme Court's actions invalidating key parts of the Voting Rights Act, the continued instances of police killings of innocent people of color, and the burning of Black churches and Muslim places of worship remind us that racism is still very alive and flourishing in the United States.

This chapter attempts to help define racism and some of the pertinent concepts involved in discussing it. The hope is that by the end of the chapter readers will have a deeper understanding about racism and the roles people can play to ensure its demise. Many of the terms and concepts introduced here are discussed more deeply throughout the book.

Defining Key Terms

Four terms that are often confused in discussions of racism are *culture*, *ethnicity*, *race*, and *nationality*. It is helpful to distinguish them.

Culture includes nonbiological characteristics of a group based on shared behaviors, thoughts, and values that are learned. Cultures often have symbols that identify them. Examples of shared culture might include hippie culture, Western culture, Middle Eastern culture, Latin culture, LGBT culture, Dallas Cowboy football culture, or racist culture.

Ethnicity also refers to social traits, not physical traits, that are shared by a human group. These traits might include a shared history, language, religion, culture, traditions, nationality, or tribe. People identify with one another as coming from common ancestors and sharing distinctive cultural traits. As opposed to race, people identify their own ethnic connection rather than it being defined and imposed by others. Some examples of ethnic groups include Native American tribes and Jews. Unfortunately, due to racism in the United States, many national, tribal, and linguistic ethnic groups have been lumped together into one single ethnic category, such as Negro, Indian, Latino, or white, which has created confusion between ethnicity and race.

Race refers to real or imagined physical traits that distinguish one group of people from another. It was first introduced in the United States as a biological concept to categorize humans based on skin color, hair texture, and eye color in order to privilege one group and to control other groups. (More on whiteness will be discussed in chapter 10.)

Nationality refers simply to one's country of citizenship. It is not an indicator of a person's race. A common mistake

Three Myths about Racism

I'm color-blind. Everyone is the same to me.
To be "color-blind" in a racialized society denies what people of color experience. To be "color-blind" is to deny the cultural values, norms, histories, and life experiences of diverse racial groups.

You only need to work hard to achieve the American dream (bootstrap mentality).
This belief does not consider the impact of racial inequality or the generational advantages some groups have, nor does it take into account circumstances pertinent to racial group membership and access to the benefits and opportunities within society.

I'm not racist. Some of my best friends are Black, Latino, Asian, etc.
Associations with individuals of other racial groups through friendship, marriage, and mission and/or volunteer work do not eliminate racist conditioning. Overcoming racism is an ongoing process.

is to ask people their nationality when what is sought is their ethnicity.

Due to this country's history of categorizing people according to skin color so that light-skinned people could have privilege, much confusion exists between how to define oneself on government forms and other documents that request information about one's identity. The racial categories most commonly used today on most applications are white, African American or Black, Hispanic/Latino, American Indian or Alaska Native, Asian, Native Hawaiian or Pacific Islander, and some other race or origin.

These categories and the high proportion of those who check "other," such as Arabs, demonstrate the development of racial identification over time, which will continue to change. Throughout the nation's history, those called white have been dominant and normative.

In 1790, as the United States began to shape its identity away from a colony and toward a nation, the first United States Congress began the process of legally codifying race with the passing of the 1790 Naturalization Act. This act limited U.S. citizenship to "free white persons of good and moral character." Not all people who were considered "white" today were seen as "white" in this period, either by legal definition or common understanding, but the passing of the 1790 act ensured that access to citizenship in the developing United States was limited to those whose ancestry was European.

Difficulty of Defining Racism

Racism is multifaceted and has both racial and cultural considerations. The complexities of racism make it nearly impossible to define as a singular concept. Although racism is informed by perceptions, attitudes, feelings, and behaviors associated with one's own racial group and other racial groups, the key factors that make racism what it is are the elements of power and privilege.

Part of the difficulty is the tendency to interchangeably define racism as *prejudice* and *discrimination*. There are differences between each of these.

Racial prejudice involves judgments, opinions, attitudes, or feelings formed before the facts are known or in disregard of the facts that contradict them related to race. We all prejudge others. Most all persons have prejudice against some other group. As long as we do not act on this prejudice to harm the other group, it is simply prejudice. Example: The belief that all members of another racial group are lazy, lack positive moral values, and are stupid.

Racial discrimination is the act or practice of giving different treatment to persons according to their membership in a racial or ethnic group. Example: A member of one racial group treats poorly or denies service to members of another racial group in a restaurant.

Prejudice and discrimination are distinguishable and describe different realities based on race with varied consequences. Most often, and for the purposes of this book, when we speak of racism we are referring to the practice of racial discrimination in which those from the dominant race are harming people from other races. The following definitions are helpful in providing a foundational understanding of racism and how racism works:

> Racism is a system of advantage or privilege based on race.
> Racism is racial prejudice plus institutional power.

In the United States and some other countries around the world, the dominant racial group is white. In the context of racism, the system of advantage or privilege primarily benefits white people. Of course, privileges and advantages do not look the same for every individual white person, due to the multiplicity of identities each person carries.

Racism in its broadest sense has particular expressions in other countries around the world. UNESCO (United Nations Educational, Scientific, and Cultural Organization) has organized a series of conferences to address issues of racism around the world. Many countries have distinct experiences of discrimination in terms of race, often negatively impacting indigenous groups, certain ethnic groups, the caste system, or immigrant groups. Because racism

Racism

Intentional and Unintentional

The personnel committee's policy is to interview members of various racial groups to meet the organization's diversity employment requirements. They continually select members of one racial group for the final candidate pool.

A teacher provides a reading list of contemporary authors to the class. The list features primarily white authors.

Overt and Covert

Members of specific racial groups are steered by a real estate agent to look only at housing in particular neighborhoods. Other clients are offered broader options.

A congregation's outsourced operating functions are always provided by individuals or businesses owned by members of one racial group.

Connected to Privilege

Some members of a college's student activities committee challenge the nomination for committee president of someone from a different racial group, stating, "We've never had a [blank] in that position, and now may not be the time."

A security guard routinely interrogates members of certain racial/ethnic groups while allowing others to simply pass by.

Connected to Power

Members of particular racial/ethnic groups are stopped while driving when they have broken no laws.

A health facility's expansion plans result in the displacement of community residents who are mostly members of one racial and economic group.

is a social construct, each country experiences it differently. In this book, the focus is on racism in the United States.

The Family of "isms"

Racism gets expressed in different ways, from patterns of access to schools, housing, employment, and health care; to language and assumptions about competency and ability; to hate crimes and violence. Racism should be "conceived as a family of *isms* based on race, or racisms."[1] Following are definitions of several types of racism and examples of each.

Individual/personal racism is an individual's belief in the superiority of her or his own racial group over other racial groups that is expressed through attitudes and behaviors that maintain those superior and inferior positions.

— A parent explains to a child that a classmate can't be as smart as she is because people in that racial group just aren't as smart as people in their own racial group.
— A worker expresses to a colleague that the new executive was hired only to meet a racial quota.
— A store manager instructs a salesperson to "keep an eye on" patrons who belong to particular racial groups.

Institutional racism includes laws, traditions, and practices that systematically result in inequalities based on racial preconceptions. It is the perpetuation of a double standard of treatment and opportunities evolving from a positive valuation of the dominant racial group (which in the United States is the group we refer to as "white") and a negative valuation of nondominant racial group members. Institutional racism may also be referred to as *systemic racism* or *structural racism*.

— A bank refuses mortgage loans for the purchase of homes in neighborhoods where mostly Latino/a, Black, and new immigrant groups reside.
— Local media coverage of an inner-city neighborhood is only about criminal activity.
— A congregation displays in its bulletins and information boards only images and cultural perspectives that reflect the dominant racial group.

Cultural racism combines elements of individual and institutional racism that express superiority or domination of one race's cultural heritage over that of another race. It is natural to have pride in one's heritage and traditions, but cultural racism comes into play when the dominant racial group holds power to define cultural values and the individual forms those values take, rewarding those who possess them and punishing or ignoring those who do not.[2] In the United States the dominant culture is white, and white people as well as people of color participate in enforcing the primacy of white culture.

— An Asian American parent prefers that her child be exposed to European classical musical forms instead of traditional Korean music in the child's diverse school.
— A Black receptionist at a medical office is noticeably agitated when communicating with patients who do not speak English.
— A school or professional sports team continues to use a Native American image as its mascot after community members have requested that it not do so.

Internalized racism involves the destructive patterns of feelings and behaviors experienced by recipients of racism when they adopt racial stereotypes, racial prejudices, and misinformation about their own racial group.[3]

— An Asian girl chooses the white Barbie doll because "she's the prettiest."
— Despite being the brightest student in class, a Latino boy chooses to sit in the back of the class and always defers to his white classmates.
— A Black worker, talking with other Black workers, insists that white people are natural leaders because they are smarter.

Environmental racism is demonstrated in the placement of toxic and hazardous waste sites, landfills, and polluting industries in Black, Asian, Latino/a, Native American, migrant worker, and working poor communities.

— A community's housing values decrease when it is discovered that the homes have been built on a toxic landfill.
— Children are experiencing symptoms of asthma and lead poisoning. A chemical plant is located in their community.
— State and city officials do not apply environmental laws, regulations, and practices uniformly across all communities.

Damages of Racism

Many who have been the targets of racism can readily express the harm of racism in their lives. What is often missed is the effect of racism on the individuals and members of groups who perpetuate it. Racism for many is defined on a personal level only. They view it as something that resides in attitudes and beliefs about one's own group's superiority and the complementary attitudes and beliefs that other groups are inferior. Some believe we simply need to concentrate on changing individual feelings, thoughts, and behaviors to eliminate racism:

> To end racism, policies must change, racist behavior must stop, the injustices from racism must be redressed, and all people must recover from the damage done to them by racism. . . . To fully eliminate racism, we must heal three forms of damage[:] . . . damage done to individuals targeted by racism[,] . . . damage to members of targeted groups from "internalized" racism . . . [and] the corruption of the minds and spirits of those conditioned by society to act as the agents of racism.[4]

Individual transformation is indeed essential. However, we must not lose sight of how racism is built into the systems that individuals live and work in.

Steps to Challenge Racism

While learning and exploring the many aspects and dimensions of racism, one might feel overwhelmed that there is so much to learn and understand. Living within a society where racism exists, we have all been affected in some way. This includes experiencing feelings of hurt, pain, anger, guilt, embarrassment, shame, or powerlessness. As Christians, we are called each day to realize God's desire for us to be in community and, through Christ's example, are encouraged to move ahead boldly. There are many concrete steps we can take. Here are just a few:

— Be open to talking about the history of your racial group and other racial groups.
— Check to see if your assumptions are based on racial stereotypes or racial prejudices.
— Be open to continuous learning to address the harm of racism.
— Recognize the privilege and power you may have based on racial group membership.
— Understand the impact your cultural values may have on others in your work and worship settings.
— Be aware of your racial prejudices and stereotypes about others.
— Appreciate the challenges and opportunities presented by perspectives from diverse racial and ethnic groups.
— Create opportunities at church, at work, and in your community to be racially diverse and inclusive.

As people of faith, we view racism as an affront to God. Racism contradicts the belief that each of us is created in the image of God, and at its basic level, racism infers that some are more valued than others in the human family.

CHAPTER 2

──────── ⌒⌒⌒ ────────

THE BIBLE AND RACISM

Does the Bible support or oppose racism? In United States history, this question has been answered both "yes" and "no." White-supremacist groups such as the Ku Klux Klan have used biblical texts as weapons to promote hatred against racial minority groups. On the other hand, some Christian traditions have used the Bible's message of liberation as a resource for the promotion of civil rights and freedom for all people. In fact, biblical themes were central to the message of the civil rights movements in the 1960s. Thus, the Bible has played a role in both promoting and dismantling racism. It has been a proof text for groups seeking to reinforce white privilege, and it has been a rich resource of empowerment for communities struggling for liberation.

This chapter addresses issues of racism in the Bible, or the extent to which race is a factor within the biblical texts themselves. It explores themes that exist within the

Hebrew Bible and the New Testament and includes a discussion of the cultural perspectives assumed within the biblical world.

Racism = Race Prejudice + Power

Race is the designation of a group of peoples based on an inherited set of phenotypical or physically identifiable traits (for example, skin color). Modern understandings of this concept emerged during the Enlightenment, coinciding with Western imperialism. As European empires expanded, they sought to classify the people whom they encountered. Hence, the idea of race is deeply rooted in colonialism. By definition, racism occurs when a particular group exerts its sense of superiority over others on account of racial difference. Therefore, racism is defined not merely as prejudice—when one race is intolerant of another—but is also related intrinsically to power, that is, the ability of a group to exercise its sense of racial dominance over others.

There are two points of discontinuity with this definition of racism and the biblical world. First, the modern notion of racism is intimately connected to developments within the last few centuries in the West, though race as a concept certainly existed earlier. Modern U.S. racism would have been an unfamiliar concept to the biblical authors. Second, ancient Israel, because of its small size and lack of power in the ancient Near East, could not have enforced its sense of superiority over other groups in a way that would resemble contemporary racism. Ancient Israel was always a small vassal state caught in the struggles of large empires such as Egypt, Assyria, Babylon, and Persia. Like all social groups, the Israelites had beliefs that reflected their own culturally limited and even ethnocentric worldview. They exhibited prejudice against other nations, but they were fairly powerless to exert their sense of group superiority in an empirewide fashion.

Early Christianity also was a minority religion during its formation in the early centuries of the Common Era. It was not until Christianity found broader acceptance within the Roman Empire that the Bible became a significant source for shaping sociocultural norms in the West. Within the context of empire, biblical themes of group superiority, which were originally generated by historically particular and geographically specific minority groups, begin to take on a more ominous tone. The language of a divinely chosen people, for example, looks much different when situated within the context of a small, colonized state or religious sect than when this belief constitutes the ideology of an empire that intends to subjugate other nations because God is on its side.

Ethnic and National Identity in the Biblical World

Within the Bible, cultural difference is not identified primarily through physical traits. The more-dominant categories were ethnicity and/or religious difference. Ethnicity is tied to a group's common cultural understanding based primarily in national origin. Ethnic groups tend to have shared understandings of the world and history. Factors such as social customs and cultural norms inform these perspectives. When biblical scholars talk about the emergence of Israel in the hill country of Canaan during the late second millennium B.C.E., they tend to focus on issues related to the rise of a small nation that emerged originally from a confederation of tribes. National identity certainly played a role in ancient Israel's self-understanding, even though the term *nation* does not correspond precisely with the contemporary notion of nation-state, which is a product of historical developments in Europe during the eighteenth century.

The table of nations in Genesis 10 and the list of Canaanite groups in Deuteronomy 7:1 point to an awareness of other nations and peoples. In the prophetic materials, the Lord's judgment is proclaimed not only on Judah and Israel but also upon the surrounding nations (Jer. 46–51 and Amos 1:1–2:3). On the surface level, the biblical texts differentiate sharply between Israelites and these foreign "others," especially those who dwell in the land of Canaan. However, biblical scholars and archaeologists have determined that the ancient Israelites were virtually indistinguishable from Canaanites. Data from archaeological artifacts and material culture support this. Moreover, biblical scholars have shown that the traditions within the Hebrew Bible have parallels with religious and mythological texts from the region. In fact, according to one theory of Israel's emergence, the Israelites were originally a loose confederation of tribes who were made up primarily of disenfranchised Canaanites. Therefore, the sharp cultural differentiation between Israelites and Canaanites in the biblical material is a social construction.

Within the Bible itself, Israel is portrayed as a culturally distinct people who are set apart from the other nations (in Hebrew, *goyim*). They were not to worship like these peoples, nor were they to make treaties or intermarry with them (Deut. 7:2–3). This language suggests that the primary way the biblical authors understood social difference was through religious beliefs and an assumed set of cultural norms.

Historical realities following the Babylonian exile informed the ideas that we find in the Bible regarding Israel and its relationship to others. Most of the biblical traditions took shape or were substantially edited within the postexilic period (late sixth and fifth centuries BCE). When the exiles returned after 538 BCE, their presence in the land was contested. These repatriating groups signaled their collective identity through sharp differentiation from the "people of the land." Hence, the biblical theme of Israel's cultural distinctiveness carries with it a particular meaning in this period. Postexilic realities also help to explain the strong tone found in the books of Ezra and Nehemiah against marriage with foreigners (Ezra 10 and Neh. 13:23–31). However, the books of Ruth and Jonah, which were also written at this time, provide a counterperspective to the xenophobic tones of Ezra and Nehemiah. Ruth is a Moabite who becomes the grandmother of King David; and the inhabitants of Nineveh, the capital of Assyria, repent and obey the Lord, unlike Jonah, the Israelite prophet. Even in these cases, however, it is clear that foreign peoples are not faithful on their own merits but are good insofar as they resemble faithful Israelites.

Within the New Testament, themes of a culturally distinct people persist. Even though the Gospel writers characterize Jesus as someone who disrupts existing social boundaries (Luke 5:30; 7:34) and challenges the religious status quo (Matt. 23:13–26; Mark 7:1–13), it is clear that the early Christians considered themselves to be uniquely situated in the world. Even in the case of Jesus, traditions exist that betray his sense of ethnic superiority. The account of the Syrophoenician (Mark 7:24–30), or Canaanite (Matt. 15:21–28), woman provides a poignant example. In this story, a woman comes to Jesus asking him to heal her daughter, who is tormented by an evil spirit. Jesus asserts that his mission is to Israel and that it would not be right for him to give the children's food to "the dogs." His juxtaposition of the term *children* to characterize his own privileged group with the ethnic slur *dogs* to designate foreigners is a shocking example of the culturally specific character of Jesus' perspective.

Though Christianity sought to extend its vision of the world to include other peoples and nations (Acts 1:8), it is clear that a culturally specific lens provided the filter for its followers' worldview. Like other Jewish groups, the early Christians maintained their identity by dividing the world into two parts: God's elect and the other nations, also known as Gentiles. In the New Testament, the Greek word for these other peoples is *ethnē*, the plural of *ethnos*, from where we get the word *ethnicity*. Hence, both the Hebrew Bible and the New Testament have a worldview that assumes a culturally and religiously distinct core of people who differentiate themselves from "foreign" groups and who have a divinely chosen role to play in the world. These chosen peoples within the Bible emerge from particular social contexts. They are minorities within much larger societies or empires.

Themes of Racism in the Bible

Though the modern concept of racism does not exist in the Bible itself, certain ideas within it resonate with contemporary social dynamics. Some trajectories lend themselves to later interpretations that both seek to justify and to resist racism.

Biblical Themes That Can Encourage Racism

Chosen people/promised land. The books of Joshua and Judges depict, in different ways, the theme of a chosen people who are called to possess a promised land. This divinely sanctioned commission includes the extermination of the previous inhabitants (see also Exod. 23:27–33; Num.

33:51–56; and Deut. 7:1–11). A key Hebrew word in this theme is *herem*, which connotes a holy thing or something dedicated to the Lord. In the case of the conquest narratives, *herem* includes the dedication of Israel's enemies and their possessions to complete destruction. This theme and its violent connotations are grounded in the central biblical idea of covenant; hence, they represent a critical way to understand God's relationship to God's people. A divinely sanctioned conquest lends itself to the possibility of racism in at least three ways: (1) the notion of a chosen people reinforces a group's sense of cultural superiority over others; (2) those who are not chosen are considered a threat to the purity of the "in" group; and (3) cultural difference is managed through the violent conquest of foreigners.

Separation from foreign others. The theme of separating from foreigners takes various forms in the Bible. It is especially prominent in the postexilic period, when groups of exiles sought to return to the land. When groups migrate, the need for clear social boundaries and identity markers becomes stronger. Within this context we find the impulse in the books of Ezra and Nehemiah to separate from foreigners, especially through the prohibition against intermarriage (Ezra 10 and Neh. 13). Foreign women are seen to be particularly threatening to the identity of the returning exilic community. Similar themes are present in the traditions about Solomon and his foreign wives (1 Kgs. 11:1–8).

The Lord's judgment on the nations. In the prophetic materials, God's judgment is often directed at the surrounding nations. Amos 1–2 uses the Lord's judgment of the nations as a rhetorical strategy to anticipate the message against Judah and Israel. Jeremiah 46–51 also contains a series of oracles against the nations. Theologically, God's wrath is intimately connected to the theme of justice. From the perspective of the biblical authors, the Lord's judgment against other nations provides a just resolution to problems in the world order. This theme universalizes the perspective of a particular group and subsumes the destiny of the world's peoples under Israel's God, who is seen as the sovereign of the earth.

Light/darkness. Another prominent theme within the biblical text relates to the symbolic idea of light overcoming darkness. In Genesis 1, God creates an ordered world out of chaos. The movement in this creation story proceeds from chaos to order, from darkness to light. This theme is also prominent in the New Testament, where it takes on connotations of enlightenment and characterizes the perspective of those who know God's salvation (John 3:19–21; Rom. 13:12; Eph. 5:8–14). This biblical metaphor, which also has strong connections with the seasons of Advent and Easter in the Christian liturgical year, implies that darkness is bad and light is good. Light overcomes darkness, and followers of the light are supposed to actively resist the darkness. In the United States, where race relations are constructed primarily within a Black/white binary, this theme contributes to configurations of meaning that support the privileging of white over Black, light over darkness.

Biblical Themes That Discourage Racism

Blessing to the nations. The Bible also contains themes that relativize or discourage racial or ethnic superiority. The promises to Abraham, for example, include not only the assurance of land and progeny but also the outcome that Abraham and his descendants will be a blessing to the nations (Gen. 12:3). Similarly, in the exilic period, Second Isaiah (Isa. 40–55) proclaims that the once-conquered people of God will be a "light to the nations" (Isa. 42:6; 49:6). In this grand vision, the prophet declares that

Israel's redemption will pave a way for all peoples so that the Lord's "salvation may reach to the end of the earth" (49:6). Israel's primary role is one of a servant whose task in the world is to be an example to the other nations.

The stranger in your midst. In the legal material of the Hebrew Bible, there is the strong charge to take care of the "stranger" (in Hebrew, *ger*) who lives in Israel (Deut. 10:17–19; Lev. 19:33–34). Moreover, the Israelites are to "love" this resident foreigner who is among them, for they themselves "were strangers in the land of Egypt" (Deut. 10:19). These passages not only encourage charity toward the *ger*, but they demand a sympathetic disposition, in which the ancient Israelites actually identify with the "other" who is among them.

Jesus' social boundary crossing. Though the Gospels depict Jesus in his cultural specificity, they also consistently characterize him as someone who challenges oppressive social structures. Jesus challenges the boundaries that serve to protect the privilege of the social elite. He encourages his followers to identify with the poor, he associates with the marginalized in society, and he challenges the ruling elite to practice justice. This aspect of Jesus' life and ministry has been influential for liberation and feminist theologians. The fight against social evils such as racism requires those who are willing to challenge existing boundaries of social convenience. Thus, Jesus serves as an example of how followers may align themselves with the oppressed of society, the marginalized whom God privileges.

There is no longer Jew or Greek. Finally, Paul's writings show an awareness of the culturally specific context of the Christian message, even as they seek to envision a new humanity that is more inclusive. In Galatians 3:28, Paul proclaims that in Christ, people are no longer "Jew or Greek." His words point toward a radical openness. However, immediately following this well-known verse,

Paul goes on to say that this vision of humanity points to the inclusion of all peoples into the promises of Abraham (3:29). Hence, Paul's vision retains elements of his own specific Jewish worldview and theology. In practice, Paul asks his followers to keep their own ethnic particularity—Jews should remain Jews, and Gentiles should stay Gentiles. His manifesto in Galatians, however, points to a common shared identity in Christ. This Pauline theme has the potential to value the diversity that is represented in the human family while pointing to elements of unity that provide common ground for people of all races and ethnicities.

Conclusion

Christians are compelled to engage the troubled past between the Bible and racism while seeking to transform the world and others through an engagement of those same biblical texts. The Bible will continue to be used to support both justice and injustice, racism and liberation. This fact does not mean that we must do away with it or hold on to some pieces of the biblical witness and leave out others. This interpretative dilemma requires us to engage simultaneously the Bible, each other, and ourselves while holding faithfully to the complexity that comes from this engagement. Doing so will help us to live into the words of Micah 6:8: "He has told you, O mortal, what is good; and what does the Lord require of you but to do justice, and to love kindness, and to walk humbly with your God?"

CHAPTER 3

ᨅᨆᨇ

THE WHITE AND NONWHITE BINARY, PART 1

All history is biased. The history we learn is written frequently from the perspective of those whose ways have determined the official story. The writers of history rarely limit their work to the presentation of facts. As historian Howard Zinn states, "The historian's distortion is more than technical, it is ideological; it is released into a world of contending interests, where any chosen emphasis supports (whether the historian means to or not) some kind of interest, whether economic or political or racial or national or sexual. Furthermore, this ideological interest is presented as if all readers of history had a common interest."[1] Rarely are our collective stories concerned with truth. History, Henry Kissinger argued, "is the memory of states."[2] Winston Churchill said, "History will be kind to me, for I intend to write it myself."[3]

The storytellers of the United States are no exception. Our national stories are a mix of symbolism and hero worship that seek to shape a strong citizenry instead of a critically thinking one. We tell a glossy story of the melting pot, with different peoples entering the country and making us into a glorious oneness, or an optimistic tale of the salad bowl, with all the different peoples mixing into a beautiful and interesting multicultural nation.

Why do we tell the stories we tell? Why do we worship as heroes historical figures such as Christopher Columbus (that's the English translation of Cristóforo Colombo, believed to be his birth name), the Pilgrims, the frontier settlers, Woodrow Wilson, Andrew Jackson, and Thomas Jefferson? Why do we focus on the contributions of diverse actors and how they overcame obstacles while detaching their histories from the legacies of colonialism, genocide, and racism?

This chapter and chapter 4 explore U.S. history through the binary of who qualifies as white and who does not. It is not so simple to explain the complex histories of people of color, including indigenous/Native American people, Black people and African Americans, Latinos/as, Asian Americans, and other groups, each of which experiences racialized consequences for not being white, and the strategies for liberation differ for each racial group.[4]

We seek to identify the patterns connecting the experiences of persons in the United States who belong to racially minoritized groups. After all, racism in the United States is more than just a Black-and-white issue. The traditional dichotomous approach to understanding race obscures the fact that the United States has always been a nation of nations, diverse and complex, and white supremacy relies upon diverse and complex strategies to uphold whiteness, even if it is to the detriment of all of us.

Citizenship

In the 1790 Naturalization Act, citizenship was first established as restricted to "free white person[s] . . . of good character." This excluded indigenous peoples, indentured servants, enslaved persons, and free Blacks, and it was later applied to Asians and people from what we now call Latin America. Europeans invaded the Americas, bringing conquest and genocide, and when the new nation was established, it added insult to injury by declaring that the invaders had rights over all else.

One hundred and fifteen years after the European invasion that began with the arrival of Columbus, the English established their first trading outpost on the Virginia coast in 1607.[5] As Sydney Ahlstrom explains, "The British knew, of course, that the terrain of the future United States was already inhabited. In fact, the conversion of heathen tribes would figure prominently among the stated objectives of imperial expansion in the New World, and long-lasting stereotypes of the Indians, as well as of the newly discovered Africans, were already taking shape."[6] The white colonialists and slave traders who were the dominant social group came to view Native Americans as vanishing savages and sought their dehumanization in order to justify genocide, to take possession of their land, and to exploit their land's resources.[7]

While on his voyage to the "New World," John Winthrop, future governor of the Massachusetts Bay Colony, wrote in 1630 of the desire held by the settlers that the new colony be like a "city on a hill" to inspire the world with the possibilities of a pure Christian commonwealth.[8]

The incongruities between the settlers' Christian faith and their conquering ways were immediately apparent when John Winthrop declared the Indian lands where his colony was established a legal "vacuum" because the Indians had not "subdued" the land and therefore had only a "natural right" but not a "civil right" to it. Natural rights had no legal standing.[9] The conquest of the Americas broadly and North America specifically found the church morally compromised by its support and justification of an enterprise driven by the need of Europeans to possess, to control, and to acquire, even if the result was the systematic destruction of culture and peoples.

Enslaved Africans arrived in Jamestown in 1619, giving way to almost three centuries of dehumanizing practices that reduced Africans to property. What is unique about African chattel slavery is that these people were considered slaves for life, forced members of a large pool of free and cheap labor, and the vast profits bought through their continued enslavement were justified through a complex code built on pseudoscience and misinterpretation of Scripture that rendered the slaves as property.

The federal restriction upon citizenship was finally amended in 1870 to include "persons of African nativity or African descent."[10] The long journey for persons of African descent who had been slaves was complicated by the Constitution's definition of slaves as three-fifths of a person. The three-fifths compromise between Southern and Northern states was part of Article 1 of the Constitution, which includes this statement:

> Representatives and direct Taxes shall be apportioned among the several States which may be included within this Union, according to their respective Numbers, which shall be determined by adding to the whole Number of free Persons, including those bound to Service for a Term of Years, and excluding Indians not taxed, three fifths of all other Persons.

This "compromise" between white men in the South and the North was to preserve the union at all costs, not a reflection of principles about humanity and the value of an enslaved person. The resulting impact, of course, was constitutional reinforcement of dehumanization of enslaved persons. The compromise shaped the Electoral College such that it gave disproportionate representation to Southern states, even though enslaved persons were excluded from voting rights. The office of the president of the United States was unduly influenced by slaveholders and frequently occupied by people who owned enslaved persons. This was only nullified after the Civil War upon the passage of the Thirteenth Amendment. With ongoing suppression of the Black vote, white Southerners maintained disproportionate power in Congress and on the presidency.

Indigenous Exclusion from Citizenship

Native Americans have a tortured relationship to U.S. citizenship, with every single treaty between sovereign nations and the United States having been violated by the United States itself. President Andrew Jackson looms large in this story. Already experienced as a military man in the killing of thousands of southern Native Americans by the time he was elected president in 1829, he said in his first message to Congress, "I suggest the propriety of setting apart an ample district west of the Mississippi . . . to be guaranteed to the Indian tribes, as long as they shall occupy it."[11] This sounds generous, but it was a promise broken, and the decision was made without the consent of the people being moved. The dividing line for the district was moved farther west from the Mississippi because this law was not put into place before white settlers moved into Iowa and Wisconsin.

The Cherokee were supposed to be moved slowly over time, but when gold was discovered in Appalachia in 1838, five tribes, including the Cherokee, were rounded up and placed into camps, and then moved along the Trail of Tears, where 25 percent of the Cherokee died. Other Indians, particularly northern tribes, were also moved against their will to the territory of the Plains Indians. Many tribes who were placed on reservations were not consulted about the boundaries or locations of these reservations. Many of them were historically nomadic, but the establishment of the reservations restricted their movement. What grew in their homeland did not necessarily grow in their new reservation. The dividing line also was not kept; as white settlers, the U.S.-Mexico War, the U.S. Civil War, and other forces encroached on the Ninety-Fifth Meridian, the lands set aside for refugee Indians shrank farther. Only 30,000 Indians lived east of the Mississippi in 1844, a dramatic decrease from the 120,000 who lived there in 1820.[12] The Navajo were forced on the "Long Walk" in the 1860s, during which they marched 450 miles from their ancestral homelands into internment campus, where one-third of them died.[13]

Colonialism

As the United States spread west in its colonial expansion, white Americans began to encroach upon territory belonging to Mexicans, who had been there for generations. So many Americans were entering the territory known as Texas that the Mexican government requested an investigation into the influx.[14] Mexican citizens were divided on the presence of Americans, with some in support and some opposed. In 1830, Mexico made slavery illegal while also prohibiting any more American migration. Americans continued to cross the border as undocumented migrants. Stephen Austin, for whom the city of Austin, Texas, is named, framed the conflict as one "between a 'mongrel Spanish-Indian and negro race' and 'civilization and the Anglo-American race.'"[15] In 1836, tensions came to a head in a series of violent confrontations. American rebels barricaded themselves in the Alamo and fought an illegal war with Mexican troops. Mexican troops captured a nearby town and executed 400 Americans. In the rebuttal to this, Americans killed 630 Mexicans. Sam Houston forced General Santa Anna to hand Texas over to him as an independent republic. Prior to the beginning of the U.S.-Mexico War in 1846, and during it, American soldiers killed Mexican civilians with impunity. In 1848, the United States defeated Mexico, and the Treaty of Guadalupe Hidalgo ceded half of Mexico to the United States, which then doubled in size, now including all of California, New Mexico, Nevada, and parts of what are now Colorado, Arizona, and Utah.[16] Millions of citizens of Mexico were suddenly on U.S. territory. This was not a war between equals; the U.S. clearly considered itself the better people. Ashbel Smith declared that the "inferior must give way before the superior race."[17] Manifest Destiny thrived throughout this conquest, being used to prove that Mexicans and their descendants were unfit for the land and that Americans were meant to take over land previously inhabited by inferior races. This provided Americans with more land and a wealth of natural resources. In 1898, the United States provided the final blow to the Spanish Empire's embattled presence in the Pacific and the Caribbean, allowing the United States to add to its holdings Guam, the Northern Mariana Islands, the Philippines, Cuba, and Puerto Rico.

In the development of the white and nonwhite binary, Northern Europeans are consistently the stars. After all, it was Northern Europeans who "discovered" these lands. It was Northern Europeans who brought "civilization" and "faith." Northern Europeans decided who could be assimilated into whiteness, with those who were from other parts of Europe slowly being integrated when it was to the advantage of those of Northern European descent. The United States continues to draw a line between citizenship and not, whiteness and not, systematically advantaging some and disenfranchising others.

Subjects and Colonial Holdings

The Foraker Act in 1900 made Puerto Rican citizens into American citizens with very limited representation (a nonvoting commissioner to the U.S. House of Representatives) and imposed a civilian government designed by the United States, including a governor and executive council appointed by the U.S. president. This opened up Puerto Rico to neocolonial domination. With Puerto Rico a territory of the United States, American companies were able to move into Puerto Rico, having been given significant tax incentives to do so. However, Puerto Rican companies were not allowed to operate in the United States. The limited representation of Puerto Rico to Washington, D.C., including the ineligibility of Puerto Ricans living on the island to vote in U.S. presidential elections, allowed any opposition to policies regarding or affecting Puerto Rico by those most affected to be ignored. In the early years of the U.S.–Puerto Rico relationship, the people of Puerto Rico voted against this particular arrangement but were overruled by the U.S. Congress. This laid the groundwork for pharmaceutical companies to enter and test drugs on the population. This testing included involuntary sterilizations of many Puerto Rican women. Although American pharmaceutical companies employed Puerto Ricans, most profits did not return to the island.

Are Arabs White?

Are Arabs a race? As comedian Dean Obeidallah stated on the Axis of Evil Comedy Tour, "I used to be a white guy. After September 11, I became an Arab."[18] Arab Americans are considered white in the legal racial construction of the United States. Arabs, a classification often conflated with Muslims, have been more prominently racialized since 9/11. The post-9/11 discourse on evil by mainstream leaders conflate Islam, terrorism, and Arabs, despite efforts by Presidents George W. Bush and Barack Obama to distinguish between Islam and violent extremism. In 2004, House majority leader Tom DeLay gave a speech in which the word *evil* was used almost twenty times to describe the so-called Arab world.[19] As English professor Steven Salaita points out, *terrorism* is a "highly subjective term and its subjectivity has been used to highlight Arab violence disproportionately while comparable American and Israeli violence is disregarded."[20] Anti-Arab racism is reflected in U.S. culture in the media, popular culture, and the Bush-era discourse of the "war on terror." After 9/11, Muslim communities reported increased difficulty with securing permits to build mosques. Of course, not all Arabs are Muslim, not all Muslims are Arabs (according to the Berkley Center of Georgetown University, "Arabs comprise only about 20 percent of the world's Muslim population"),[21] and not all Arabs or Muslims are terrorists. In fact, adherents of Islam span a wide theological and political spectrum, similar to the spectrum of practicing Christians. This conflation in the American imagination of Arab/Muslim/terrorist creates a racialized category whose members are assumed to participate in destructive behavior.

After September 11, 2001, hate crimes against people who looked Arab increased dramatically. Between September 11 and September 13, the Council on American-Islamic

Relations received over three hundred reports of harassment and abuse. The first murder was of a South Asian man in Arizona, believed to have been targeted because of his turban and long beard, which are characteristic of Sikh adherents.[22]

The aftermath of September 11 included voluntary registration by men from twenty majority-Muslim and majority-Arab countries.[23] These voluntary registrations resulted in hundreds of men disappearing for months at a time, thanks to the government's "hold until cleared" policy.[24] Many were deported, and most were held in detention without the ability to contact their families.

Hispanic, Non-Hispanic

The first time the U.S. Census attempted to count people based on Hispanic ethnicity was 1970, during the Nixon administration.[25] The question about Hispanic ethnicity has complicated the conversation about whiteness and Hispanic identity. Everyone is asked if they are of Hispanic ethnicity, and every person who identifies as Hispanic is also asked their race, leaving no clear option for those who experience their racial identity as Hispanic/Latino. And the racialization of people who are Hispanic or Latino makes it clear that whiteness is conditional and attached to citizenship, with even those who have been in the United States as a result of the country gobbling up their ancestral lands suspected of not being American. The debate regarding immigration reform and enforcement has cycled through both cultural and systemic racism. Vigilantes on the border between the United States and Mexico engage in anti-Latino violence, believing they are assisting the U.S. Border Patrol in finding and turning back people crossing the border. Since 1994, border enforcement and the construction of a wall along portions of the U.S.-Mexico border have forced immigrants into more hazardous terrain. Such measures have made these crossings more dangerous, and those who cross successfully are more likely to stay longer and to bring their families, because going home for a visit is now far more difficult.[26] The naturalization process involves quotas that do not reflect colonial histories or current flows of migration. Colonization has resulted in later immigration of previous colonial subjects (e.g., Indian and Pakistani migration to Great Britain, Filipino migration to the United States). Quotas have fluctuated, with limits placed on per-country immigration and varying based on hemisphere of origin, replaced with overall annual limits.

In contrast to the sunny view of the beautiful long-standing diversity of the United States, this reading of history from the perspective of who is considered white and not white demonstrates how deeply racialization has shaped the experiences of Americans throughout history. In fact, it is such a powerful force that it has even shaped the experiences of people around the world impacted by the American racialized view of their countries.

CHAPTER 4

THE WHITE AND NONWHITE BINARY, PART 2

The qualifications for naturalization were fundamentally changed in 1870. The Fourteenth Amendment to the Constitution, ratified in July 1868, states, "All persons born or naturalized in the United States, and subject to the jurisdiction thereof, are citizens of the United States and of the State wherein they reside." However, even after the ratification of the Fourteenth Amendment and the passing of the 1870 Naturalization Act that included "persons of African nativity or African descent" as eligible for citizenship, other people of color were left in quite a bind. Many Asians approached naturalization by arguing that they were either "free white persons" or of "African descent." In 1922–1923, the Supreme Court heard cases from a Japanese immigrant and an Indian immigrant, both of whom argued they were "free white persons." Takao Ozawa, a Japanese citizen, wrote a brief outlining the ways in which he was American (his marriage, his disaffiliation with anything Japanese, his Christian faith) and also argued that his skin was white.

The Supreme Court ruled against him, citing that "Caucasian" and "white" were the same and that since Ozawa was not Caucasian, he could not be white.[1] Deciding to use this ruling of "Caucasian" as a qualifying factor, Bhagat Singh Thind referred to the science of the day. Social scientists placed Asian Indians within the Caucasoid region and also stated they were Aryan. Despite the Supreme Court's ruling of a few months before, the court decided to ignore its own equation of Caucasian and white and held that "the words 'free white person' are words of common speech, to be interpreted in accordance with the understanding of the common man."[2] The decision went on to say that Thind could not be considered white according to the understanding of "the common man."

While Asians are now eligible for naturalization, the "perpetual foreigner" stereotype ensures that even native-born citizens of Asian descent continue to experience that citizenship as conditional. Whenever conflict, economic or diplomatic, rears its head between the United States and an Asian nation, Asian Americans suffer the consequences. Vincent Chin was murdered by two white autoworkers in Detroit when Japanese cars became wildly popular and the U.S. auto industry was suffering. Asian Americans faced skyrocketing levels of hate speech and racialized violence during the COVID-19 pandemic. Additionally, restrictions on immigration through the visa system make it difficult for Asians to immigrate and become naturalized, with some populations experiencing dramatically long wait times. People of Asian descent are told they are "proximal to whiteness" but experience consistently that they are not white.

Japanese Concentration Camps

The bombing of Pearl Harbor by Japanese warplanes shocked and outraged the American people—and led to another shameful period of forced migration and segregation. Anti-Japanese hysteria led to a number of organizations—such as the American Legions of California, Oregon, and Washington; the *Los Angeles Times*; and the Grower-Shipper Vegetable Association—to call for the removal of all those of Japanese descent.[3]

Attorney General Francis Biddle stated in a memo to President Franklin Roosevelt that evacuation of American citizens based on their racial categorization was determined to be unconstitutional.[4] In February 1942, FBI Director J. Edgar Hoover determined that Japanese in the United States and Japanese Americans posed no real espionage threat. Despite this counsel, President Roosevelt signed Executive Order 9066 on February 19, 1942. General John DeWitt was authorized to remove all Americans of Japanese descent from the Western states to be processed and relocated to inland concentration camps. Approximately 120,000 persons—men, women, and children—were moved from their homes. The United States also requested that Latin American governments deport over 2,200 persons of Japanese descent from Latin America to the United States to be interned and used for prisoner exchanges.[5] Families were told they had just a few days to sell all their belongings or entrust them to banks, friends, or neighbors. The shame of being seen as the enemy was multiplied as white people came to buy valuables, houses, and land for far less than their actual value. Despite the Alien Land Laws, which prohibited noncitizen ownership of land in the western United States, Japanese American families managed to own or lease some lucrative farmland that was highly coveted by neighboring white farmers, producing 40 percent of all vegetables grown in California. The Farm Security Administration transferred ownership of many Japanese American farms to Dust Bowl refugees or naturalized immigrants from Europe.[6] Imprisonment was "'partially initiated by California corporate agribusiness interests hoping to satisfy their own lust for land while ridding themselves of competition from the state's most productive family farms.'"[7] Entire families left everything, bringing only what they could carry. They went first to evacuation centers and then to assembly centers. These assembly centers were in the horse and cattle stalls at such places as the fairgrounds in Puyallup, Washington, and the Santa Ana racetrack in California, made famous by Seabiscuit. They then were sent to live for three years in uninsulated barracks in various rural areas, where the family system was severely disrupted by a life without private space. People were not allowed to leave the camps unless accompanied by guards while providing labor to neighboring farms, or unless they were on their way to serve in the military. In contrast, the only people of German and Italian descent imprisoned within the United States were those charged with specific acts of espionage.

The Limits of Citizenship

Even citizens were disqualified from whiteness, or the rights pertaining to white persons. Jim Crow laws were put into place throughout the colonial era and increased in the North after most slavery there was abolished. These laws were firmly established in the South after Reconstruction.[8] Jim Crow segregation was accepted in the North, and in the South it was clearly labeled, thanks to "whites only" signs posted over separate entrances, drinking fountains, and restrooms. Segregation continued in the North after World War II through the practice of restrictive covenants, agreements put in place by homeowners pledging never to sell their property to certain people (typically Jews and people from nonwhite racial groups).

The Supreme Court decision *Plessy v. Ferguson* in 1896 established the legality of "separate but equal" places of transportation, and thereby educational and other social institutions. This left Jim Crow in place, under the obviously false premise that resources were distributed equally between white and Black segments of the population. In spite of this, and persistent inequities, Black colleges and universities persevered in their commitment to providing higher education. The Supreme Court decision *Brown v. Board of Education* in 1954 struck down *Plessy v. Ferguson*, establishing that separate is not equal. A key piece of evidence was a study done observing the impact of segregation on the self-image of Black girls. They were presented with a white doll and a Black doll and asked which was pretty, which was good, and which was bad. The Black girls chose the white doll as the pretty and good doll and the Black doll as the bad doll. *Brown v. Board of Education* ended an era of legal segregation by race and laid the groundwork for the slow work of integrating a firmly segregated population.

After World War II ended, several factors resulted in the development of a white middle class in a way that left Black people, in particular, behind. (The status of Latinos/as, Asian Americans, and Native Americans varied according to location and is less well documented.) What took place before the end of legal segregation laid the foundation for continued exclusion of Black people after 1954, further cementing inequality that arose not out of intent but from the continued impact of historical racism.

Congress passed the G.I. Bill at the end of World War II, providing such benefits as subsidized education and homeownership assistance to all veterans of the war. However, the ability of veterans to take advantage of the bill's provisions varied according to race. White working-class and lower-class men were able to move up to the middle class thanks to subsidized higher education. Black men were unable to do the same, since educational opportunities were curtailed by legal segregation that allowed universities to refuse admission to Black applicants. This inability to obtain an education as easily as white men was compounded by obstacles to purchasing a home, the primary way in which people in the United States have been able to accrue wealth that can be passed down to succeeding generations.

As soldiers returned from service and settled down in homes and with families, white flight began with a vengeance. Whites were able to move out to the burgeoning suburbs thanks to a number of factors. The first was lending practices that privileged white applicants over Black applicants. Redlining (the practice by which banks drew lines on maps between neighborhoods to delineate those neighborhoods in which they would lend money to buyers to purchase houses) and restrictive covenants (in which buyers agreed not to sell their house to anyone from such groups as Jews, Black people, or Asians) cemented residential segregation. Whites were able to move out to the suburbs. Black people were led to city residences, Black suburbs, or particular lower-value neighborhoods by a practice called steering. Steering takes place when real estate agents show prospective buyers only certain houses, a practice that persists. Until the 1980s, blockbusting contributed to residential segregation, as real estate agents encouraged white homeowners to sell their houses as Black families began moving into a particular neighborhood, citing the likelihood that home values would fall as a result of integration.

Growth of the suburbs was encouraged by the further development of interstate highways, which were first built on a large scale during the Cold War to move military equipment and people safely across distances. As the interstates developed, more suburban growth took place as a result of easier movement between cities and their suburbs. Urban renewal—a term used to describe Black displacement, interstate development, and the destruction of viable communities—allowed this movement between (largely white) suburbs and (largely Black) urban cores. As Tom Lewis notes, James Baldwin "characterized urban renewal more caustically as 'Negro removal.'"[9] The Riverfront Expressway in New Orleans effectively turned a family-friendly, economically vibrant Black community— and the center of Black Mardi Gras in New Orleans—into the street below the elevated Interstate 10. By the early 1960s, it became clear that the way of least resistance for interstate construction was a Black community, as residents did not have sufficient access to city government and its power structure to fight these developments. Highway engineer Robert Moses "each year leveled the homes of tens of thousands of blacks to make way for ever more miles of expressways around and through New York."[10]

The G.I. Bill, white flight and the housing boom, the expansion of higher education to more working-class and lower-class white men, and legal segregation laid the groundwork for a booming white middle class and a Black community without access to the same benefits, further entrenching inequality between Black and white. The outcomes of these laws and practices endure into the twenty-first century, resulting in racist outcomes of institutional policies not intended to be racist. David Roediger quotes *Ebony* magazine's analysis of a Frank Sinatra movie called *The House I Live In*, about white immigrants who organized around issues of homeownership and discrimination:

"Never will a white man in America have to live in a ghetto hemmed in by court-approved legal documents, trapped by an invisible wall of hate much more formidable than the Siegfried line."[11]

Criminalization and Legalized Disenfranchisement

The last legal obstacles to full citizenship for Black people were eliminated with the 1965 Voting Rights Act, a key provision of which was overturned in 2013 by the U.S. Supreme Court.[12] Citizenship implies full participation in society, including voting. This is not possible for many people who have been convicted of felonies. Almost 25 percent of all Black men in their thirties had been to prison by 2003; 1 out of every 13 Black people are ineligible to vote due to felony convictions.[13] In addition, Black people receive longer prison sentences for drug crimes because sentencing varies based not on the crime committed but on the ways in which people of different races are charged (with possession, or with possession with the intent to distribute) and on the types of drugs. For example, crack cocaine is cheaper and more likely to be used by Black people than powder cocaine, which is more likely to be used by white people. Under a 1986 sentencing act, users of powder cocaine need to possess 100 times more cocaine than do users of crack cocaine in order to receive the same sentence, reduced to an 18-to-1 ratio in the 2010 Fair Sentencing Act. Because of the differences in sentencing over time, the impact of incarceration has been much greater on poor people of color from urban areas.[14]

The criminal justice system impacts the way Black people in particular experience citizenship. Convicted felons who have served their time in prison and completed probation remain ineligible to vote in most states. Only Maine and Vermont allow prison inmates the right to vote.[15]

Thirty-five states prohibit felons on parole from voting. Florida voters approved the extension of voting rights to former felons in 2018, but implementation has dragged thanks to the state's governor. Given the disproportionate numbers of Black and Latino men in prison, and the disproportionate sentences given to people of color, we might say that the result of these laws is the restriction of citizenship based on race. We also see how Black and indigenous people experience dehumanization through disproportionately high rates of death as a result of interactions with police.

Conclusion

The line between white and nonwhite is persistent throughout U.S. history, with white ethnic immigrants typically experiencing assimilation into whiteness, ensuring an enduring white majority, with some exceptions. Even those forced to choose "white" on the census, such as Middle Easterners and Arab Americans and some Hispanics, do not experience whiteness in the same way that others do. White Jews faced growing incidents of violence and hatred during the Trump era, singled out for religion even while carrying what may be considered other markers of whiteness. And those who are not white continue to experience racism, bigotry, limited opportunity, structural oppression, and marginalization.

Viewed through this lens, U.S. history appears less a glorious multicultural salad bowl and more a multifaceted locus of oppression and resistance.

CHAPTER 5

TRUMPISM

During the Obama presidency, shiny visions were presented of the United States becoming a country evenly split between people of color and white people, or even a majority-minority country (where people of color would eventually outnumber white people) by 2040.[1] Any idealized notions of racial progress were effectively dashed by the candidacy of Donald Trump and his subsequent election. By some accounts, the Trump campaign was almost as surprised by the win as the rest of the country, and as a result unprepared for governance. Trump's rise accompanied a growing visibility of police violence and brutality against indigenous Americans, but most especially against Black Americans for such alleged crimes as trying to leave a traffic stop, breaking down on the road, selling loose cigarettes, being pulled over while carrying a legally permitted firearm, or playing with a toy gun. All too often these encounters with the police resulted in death. Trump's term as president saw the usual white supremacist structures become the architectural support for a refreshed wave of white nationalism, a flashback to prior presidential administrations where blatant racism became policy, with increased rates of hate crimes and racist rhetoric.[2]

White Identity Politics

Many might find the discussion of the Trump administration's legitimization of white nationalism and white supremacy uncomfortable. However, the overall impact of the administration's policies, the unceasingly dangerous rhetoric that originated from the Trump White House, and the campaign and presidency's endorsement by such white nationalists as David Duke make it clear that the United States must face up to many hard truths about the Trump era and its lasting effects.

When Donald Trump entered the presidential race in 2015, the tenor of the changing nature of white supremacy in the United States came to the surface. What was considered by many to be a fringe movement of conspiracy theorists and anti-Muslim birthers revealed itself to align easily with a broad coalition of single-issue pro-life voters, white supremacists and nationalists, fiscal conservatives, and white evangelicals. While not every Trump voter was a Trump supporter, and not every Trump supporter was enraged by social and cultural changes in recent U.S. history, at least part of Trump's appeal was his ability to tap into the seething resentment at those changes. The ongoing concern with the rise of Donald Trump is not fully or even mostly about the individual himself (although it is easy to focus on him). The problem is with what has been called Trumpism, a form of right-wing populism fueled by the backlash to cultural change. According to Ben Tarnoff, Trumpism has two components: "the notion that people of color and women are less than fully human" and "an anti-elite ethos that pairs a critique of corporate oligarchy with support for a degree of social protection."[3]

The result in 2016 was majority-white support for the Trump-Pence ticket, with a much broader coalition supporting the Clinton-Kaine ticket, which won the popular vote but lost the Electoral College. Investigations revealed Russian interference in the 2016 election, tipping in Trump's favor, and it became clear how the path to the White House was paved through stories of voter suppression at the state level and the effect of the gutting of the Voting Rights Act.[4] As Carol Anderson lays out in the afterword to the paperback edition of her book *White Rage*, one enormous impact of the Republican commitment to curtailing voting rights and access was the election of Donald Trump to the office of the president and the subsequent crumbling of democratic institutions.[5] As a result, hard-won protections for civil and human rights for people of color, sexual minorities, and transgender people were rolled back.

For all the hand-wringing about "identity politics" shaping or driving the policies of the Democratic Party, white identity politics appear to have driven Trump's Republican Party. In *Dying of Whiteness* by Jonathan Metzl, the author's research on repealing gun control laws in Missouri, gutting public services in Kansas, and limiting healthcare access in Tennessee demonstrates that in many cases the perception that nonwhite people, and especially Black people, would benefit from a particular policy drove many white people to oppose the policy, even when that policy benefited them as well.[6] They would rather die, literally and figuratively, than allow people of color to have access to healthcare or education.

White Supremacy and
White Nationalism

White supremacy is the ideology that what is white is superior. It is built into the structures and culture of the United States and is internalized by the most well-meaning of people without their knowledge or consent.

White nationalism (as embodied by the 2017 "Unite the Right" march in Charlottesville, Virginia) seeks to expel migrants and "cleanse" the nation of people of color, justifying these actions on the basis of white genetic superiority. Stephen Ray, a theologian and president of Chicago Theological Seminary, sums up the distinction in this way:

> White Supremacy is a system of thought and material relations predicated on the idea that white people ought [to] have the right of first refusal on the common goods of our society.
>
> White Nationalism is a system of thought and material relations predicated on the idea that white people ought to have exclusive claim on the goods of our society. . . . A system of white supremacy only requires that non-white people know their place in the social order. In a system of white nationalism there is no place for non-white people.[7]

While there is no question that white supremacy has been part and parcel of U.S. society and government throughout its history, during the Trump administration white nationalism returned with a vengeance. Often known as belonging to the "Alt-Right," a term coined by Richard Spencer, white nationalists adhere to a narrative of white grievance, support policies of cultural genocide, seek to roll back civil rights gains, and promote anti-Semitism and Islamophobia. White nationalists had representation in the White House with presidential advisor Steve Bannon, whose website for right-wing news and community, Breitbart, provides a platform for the Alt-Right, and advisor Stephen Miller, who authored much of the administration's immigration policy.

During the Trump administration, the mix of the United States' toxic masculinity and its obsession with underregulated access to firearms led to mass shootings at synagogues in Pittsburgh in 2018 and in Poway, California, in 2019, and to another mass shooting at a Walmart in El Paso, Texas, targeting Latinos during back-to-school shopping in 2019. At the Charlottesville rally in August 2017, a white Black Lives Matter protester was killed by the driver of a car who drove into protesters. This pattern of motorists driving into groups of protestors increased particularly in 2020.

Xenophobia and Isolationism

Trump launched his campaign for president in June 2015, saying Mexican immigrants "[are] bringing drugs. They're bringing crime. They're rapists. And some, I assume, are good people."[8] This inauspicious beginning demonstrated that racist xenophobia would become a dominant theme of the Trump administration, manifesting in:

— a ban on migration from several majority-Muslim countries upheld by the Supreme Court despite early strong citizen-led resistance;
— an almost complete overhaul of how refugee applications were processed, slowing the flow of refugees admitted to the U.S. to a trickle (a ceiling of 110,000 under the Obama administration dropped to 18,000 under the Trump administration in FY 2020) despite

the worldwide number of refugees reaching an all-time high since World War II;[9]

— an acceleration of deportations and escalation to deportations of noncriminals;

— new policies mandating separation of families upon entry to the United States, holding children arriving alone in detention centers instead of placement with family members or foster homes;

— ongoing growth of detentions, with the added layer of Trump administration officials determining eligibility of pregnant minors to access abortion care, including tracking the menstrual cycles of minors to monitor potential pregnancy status, presumably to block their access to abortion;[10]

— detained immigrants being given hysterectomies without informed consent, leaving them sterilized at a Georgia detention center;[11]

— refusal to allow arrivals seeking asylum to enter the country and be processed promptly, instead creating massive unsafe and unsanitary camps of people fleeing their countries just across the border in Mexico;

— consideration of new regulations no longer allowing H4 visa holders to work (H4 visas are granted to spouses of H1B visa holders who are highly specialized workers, and disproportionately Indian and Chinese women);

— ongoing efforts to end Deferred Action for Childhood Arrivals (DACA);

— an extensive trade war with China;

— holding China responsible for the COVID-19 pandemic, calling the coronavirus the "China virus";

— withdrawal of the United States from the World Health Organization, from the Paris Accords, and from the agreement with Iran, and antagonizing Iran, and other disruptions to diplomatic relations akin to increased isolationism;

— attacks on the critical race theory framework as "ideology" and a declaration that racial sensitivity trainings are "un-American," including an order to the Office of Management and Budget to terminate government contracts for such training.[12]

White Protestant (mainline and evangelical) support for the administration persisted even though it declined somewhat during the COVID-19 pandemic. To cement this support, the Trump administration targeted causes close to the hearts of many white Protestants, such as refugee resettlement. At the same time, significant majorities of nonwhite Protestants, specifically Black and Hispanic, disapproved of Trump.[13]

During the Trump years, the gulf between the racial attitudes of white Christians and nonwhite Christians was deep on a number of specific issues. Research by the Public Religion Research Institute in 2019 revealed this:

More than three-quarters of white Christians overall—including 83 percent of white evangelicals, 75 percent of white Catholics, and 71 percent of white mainline Protestants—believe that racial minorities use racism as an excuse for economic inequalities more than they should. . . . Only 30 percent of Black Protestants agree.[14]

White Christians were much more likely than religiously unaffiliated white people, at 52 percent, to doubt the existence of structural injustice.

Pandemic and Race

The novel coronavirus arrived in the United States in 2020 as the presidential race was heating up. The impact of the COVID-19 pandemic on racial attitudes and on people of color in the United States was dramatic. Trump persistently used the phrase "the Chinese virus," and Asian Americans experienced discrimination against their businesses, particularly Chinese restaurants, because the virus is believed to have begun in China. Moreover, Asian Americans experienced an enormous increase in anti-Asian violence, according to Stop AAPI Hate, which documents hate crimes and incidents against Asian Americans and Pacific Islanders.

By three months into the pandemic, indigenous, Black, and Latino/a communities were already experiencing higher rates of infection and death.[15] By the summer of 2020, twice as many Filipino healthcare workers had died in the United States as in the Philippines, due to COVID exposure.[16] Additionally, indigenous tribes saw aid delayed by the Trump administration.[17] Communities suffering from chronic underfunding, particularly indigenous communities, struggled to keep pace with the pandemic. The anemic short-term response to the pandemic propelled people whose livelihoods were impacted by shutdowns and stay-at-home orders into increasingly precarious economic situations, with disproportionate impacts on Latino/a, Black, and indigenous households.[18]

Police violence against Black men came to the fore with the murder of George Floyd on May 25, 2020. Video taken showed Floyd pinned to the ground by multiple officers, with one officer kneeling on his neck for nine minutes and thirty seconds.[19] He died as a result. Uprisings around the country exploded, even in the face of the pandemic. Communities marched, largely masked, demanding justice for George Floyd and others, such as Breonna Taylor of Louisville, Kentucky, who was shot by police executing a no-knock warrant when looking for a suspect who was already in custody. These protests energized a significant portion of the population, and resulting changes included Louisville ceasing to use no-knock warrants, more than 130 Confederate statues and other symbols of historic and controversial figures seen as racially unjust being removed in cities across the country,[20] corporations of all sorts proclaiming their support of Black Lives Matter for the first time, and other work toward reform of policing and community engagement.

Religious communities were among those motivated to address racial justice issues. Antiracism trainers and speakers found themselves inundated with requests.[21] Racist behavior caught on camera had begun to face consequences, thanks to social media, and the desire for accountability seemed to increase in the urgency of 2020.

Conclusion

The midterm elections of 2018 and the presidential election of 2020 demonstrated strong opposition, especially among people of color, to the racism and xenophobia of the Trump administration and the ongoing vitality of Trumpism. In 2018 the most diverse electorate to date chose from among the most diverse pool of candidates to date. The midterm elections flipped the House of Representatives from majority Republican to majority Democratic, as voting among all people of color groups became even more Democratic.[22] For the 2020 presidential election, the Democratic Party saw the most diverse field of candidates to date. The election to the vice presidency of Kamala Harris, the first Black woman and woman of South Asian descent to achieve that office, pointed to the strength of a diverse coalition of voters.

During the 2020 Republican National Convention, the Trump administration and the Republican Party seemed driven to present a face to the nation to assure their base that a vote for Trump was not racist or sexist. A diverse group of speakers played a role in the convention. But those in opposition to Trump did not forget the impact of the administration. After all, Trump had a portrait of Andrew Jackson, the driving force behind the Indian Removal Act, hung in the White House. And with record turnout supporting both candidates, with an overwhelming majority (by both the popular vote and the Electoral College), Trump was voted out. He and his supporters sought to overturn the results by whipping up populist sentiment and filing lawsuits around the country, seeking to disenfranchise voters, with particular attacks on areas with Black voters. The most alarming manifestation of the impact of the lies spread by Trump and his allies undermining the validity of the election was the January 6, 2021, invasion of the Capitol during the Congressional vote to certify the 2020 Presidential election results. Armed insurrectionists responded to Trump's urging at a rally and stormed the Capitol, successfully (if temporarily) interrupting the vote, terrorizing lawmakers, staff, and journalists carrying out the business of the government, and wreaking destruction and havoc. Trumpism may not hold the popular sway as once feared, but it continues to be widespread and extremely dangerous to the highest ideals of the United States.

PART II

ISSUES OF
RACISM TODAY

CHAPTER 6

〰️

COLONIALISM, IMMIGRATION, AND ASSIMILATION

R acism is a political and social construct that intersects every aspect of our lives as a community. No academic discipline or lived experience escapes the pervasiveness of racism and white supremacy. Colonialism and immigration are two of the points at which racism and human economic, social, and historical life intersect. They stem directly from U.S. and Western European politics of expansion. The interconnectedness between colonialism and immigration is also present in the life, mission, and witness of the U.S. church. One of the most vibrant and increasingly present expressions of the church in the United States is migrant congregations. Migrants arrive in the United States in pursuit of freedom, political stability, economic opportunity, and social belonging. Many migrants bring a deep engagement with the faith of Jesus, one they learned from historic or contemporary missionizing endeavors. By and large, the members of these migrant communities also have a deep commitment to the U.S. expression of their tradition. Is the U.S. institutional church welcoming the perspective and vibrancy these communities bring? Are members of the U.S. institutional church expecting these communities to conform to "our" way? It is important to be aware of the pervasiveness of racism in U.S. political, social, cultural, and religious institutions. To respond to this sinful reality, U.S. Christians should identify the root causes of racism. Christians also ought to articulate the ways our institutional, theological, and missionary witnesses have benefited from, participated in, and encouraged racism. In the next few pages we invite you to delve a little deeper into the United States' political and religious history of colonialism — in its expansionist endeavors and its relation with current migrant movements into the United States and with the country's immigration policy.

Racism and Colonial Expansion

What led Queen Isabel of Castile to fund Columbus's exploration enterprise in 1492 is more complex than a simple rush from having conquered the last Muslim kingdom of the Iberian Peninsula in 1491.[1] A child of the Reconquista, Isabel was an heir of the centuries-old narrative that Christians deserved, by providence, the land occupied by the other — usually the religious and ethnic other.[2] This ideology goes all the way back to the Crusades, and the Reconquista was only one expression of it. Less than two years after the Reconquista, Pope Alexander VI published *Inter caetera*, a papal bull that emboldened Portugal's economic interests in West Africa (with connections to the development of the transatlantic trade of enslaved Africans), Spain's political ambitions of territorial expansion (which led to its violent conquest of most of the Americas), and England's desire to extend its reach beyond Ireland (which led to the violent conquest of North America). *Inter caetera* is one of the most influential of a series of papal bulls in the fifteenth century that gave the political, economic, legal, and theological grounding for what we now know as the Doctrine of Discovery.[3]

After independence, the United States continued in the tradition of the Doctrine of Discovery. As an internal affairs policy, Manifest Destiny set the ideological stage for the political aim for the United States to reach the Pacific Coast. Manifest Destiny, however, was far more than the purchase of the Louisiana Territory, the annexation of Texas and Oregon in 1846, and the settling of most of the northern territory of Mexico by 1848.[4] Manifest Destiny was the ideology by which the United States sought war with its neighbors to achieve its expansionist agenda.[5] It was also the ideology by which the financial interests of a subset of the population were deemed the top priority, to the point of deploying the armed forces of the United States to accomplish them. Manifest Destiny intersects the reality of the enslaved population through the politicizing of the Missouri Compromise. Manifest Destiny also meant the intentionally bloody displacement and abhorrent massacre of Native American nations, and the exploitation of sacred lands. The abuse of the environment was catastrophic — plowing through a transcontinental rail system and the unhinged extraction of gold, oil, and other natural resources. The consequences of Manifest Destiny on the groups of people it marginalized are still lived today.

The international incarnation of the U.S. continuation of the Doctrine of Discovery was the Monroe Doctrine.[6] The end of the first quarter of the 1800s was a time of major independence movements throughout the Caribbean and Latin America. "America for the Americans" is a way to summarize the ideology behind these movements. It communicated to European powers that at a time when many countries throughout the Caribbean and Latin America were achieving independence, any intention to constitute new European colonies in the region would be understood as an act of aggression against the United States. Although as a young republic at the time the United States was not thought to have had the power to enforce the Monroe Doctrine, the checkered relations between the United States and Latin America are framed through the doctrine. The doctrine proved to be more of an opportunity to encourage and protect U.S. economic and political interests in the Western Hemisphere.

The ideology that gave us the Doctrine of Discovery, Manifest Destiny, and the Monroe Doctrine is one in which marginalization, oppression, and disenfranchisement are acted upon people who do not conform to the standards of the dominant group. This ideology props up the idea of the supremacy and privilege of the dominant group. Supremacy and privilege are always over and against the othered groups. A way in which supremacy and dominion are enacted is by the engineering of categories (e.g., race, ethnicity, culture, gender). We have been taught that the victors are the ones who write history. What is more, that history is written from the social perspective, the historical standpoint, and the political method of empire. That method usually includes the artificial fragmentation of the historical narratives of the oppressed. In the Antillean archipelago of the Caribbean, in spite of the geographic, historical, and cultural proximity of the peoples of these islands, language has been used to keep people, stories, and histories apart.[7] The intention of state officials in Arizona to ban ethnic studies in the school curriculum, or Texas education officials seeking to call enslaved Africans "workers" are only two more recent examples of how official (imperial) history intentionally silences, makes invisible, and downright crushes whole groups of people.[8] This silencing occurs in history books and legislation imposed upon groups of people. Jesus' example provides an alternative to the actions and impositions of empire: listening to and sharing stories. Himself a member of a marginalized group by empire, Jesus spent his ministry being present to everyone he encountered, from crowds to Samaritan and Syrophoenician women. In being countercultural, these encounters were also political acts. Discovering that which we hold in common questions the narratives we have been taught and opens our minds and hearts to discovering that the artificial fragmentations we experience are just that—artificial.

These acts of fragmenting, and the downright erasing of the culture and history of marginalized people, are also political and financial. The history written by empires frames the metanarratives in the service of those empires. It intentionally excludes stories that connect the history of struggle and survival of marginalized peoples. U.S. and European tellings of the history of the Caribbean Islands, for instance, intentionally ignores the connections of the Haitian Revolution with the Dominican War of Independence; the Spanish repression in Cuba and Puerto Rico; the British strong arm in Jamaica, St. Lucia, and Trinidad and Tobago; and the revolutionary organizing happening in Caracas, Venezuela. Over a century later, we see how Caribbean regional relations are tainted along the demarcations (political, social, and economic) imposed from Washington, Paris, Madrid, London, and Amsterdam.[9] We also see how this metanarrative continues to inform policies from the United States and Western European powers with their political and economic subordinates. The current relationships between the United States and Haiti and Cuba are good examples. After sixty years of an economic blockade designed to purportedly suppress the communist regime in Cuba, the Obama administration began to ease diplomatic relations. The plan was that enhancing economic, cultural, educational, and political engagement with Cuba would encourage the exchange of American democratic values. Five years later, under the Trump administration, the embargo tightened again, and the people of Cuba are the ones left to suffer the consequences.[10] The openness in relations that created a boom of entrepreneurship throughout the country was shut down almost immediately with the stroke of a pen—simply because the United States could. The political and economic turmoil in Haiti has been part of its existence since independence. Per the metanarrative told by Paris and Washington, such turmoil occurs because of corruption found in every government of the republic.

What is not said in the imperial metanarrative about Haiti is that as a result of independence, France submitted Haiti to crushing terms to fulfill its external debt.[11] Neither is it widely shared that the United States invaded the country twice (1915 and 1994) to protect U.S. economic interests.[12] If you combine financial submission, military and political imposition, and hurricanes and earthquakes, you can understand the desire of Haitians of all walks of life to seek a better economic and political status for themselves. Haitian migration is a result of the multiple interventions of the United States in Haitian affairs for the sake of U.S. interests. And yet U.S. restrictive immigration policy is put in place to prop up U.S. political interests.[13] Despite the contributions of migrants to the economic, social, cultural, and political fabric of the United States, most of them (including those with temporary protected status) are treated as expendable. Even when there is proof that returning to their countries of origin will place their livelihoods (and often their lives) in danger, policies are enacted without consideration of how U.S. policies and interests caused the migration of these peoples in the first place. The metanarrative tells an imperial story. The meta-narrative silences the histories of many.

The way the history is written also shows how policies are crafted. And often the policies imposed seek to protect U.S. and Western European financial interests. As far back as the nineteenth century, some of the interests that sought to be protected were the payment for lost property. In this case we are referring to the reimbursement for the loss of capital due to the freeing of slaves after the triumph of the Haitian Revolution and the subsequent abolition of slavery in the rest of the region. Policies were put in place to make sure landowners had the capital to pay off mortgages and compensate for the loss of income from agricultural specu-lation.[14] Other interests protected by policies of Western powers, especially of the United States (in the Caribbean and throughout the Western Hemisphere) include the access to raw materials (including agricultural and mining) and intellectual capital (access to a well-educated, mostly nonunion, lower-cost labor pool), while undermining democracy, financial autonomy, and political sovereignty.

The Colonialist Roots of Immigration Policy

Colonialism and racism serve to advance the supremacy of a particular people. Those who are victims of this exploi-tation will inevitably seek places where they can more freely pursue liberty, well-being, and prosperity. And the movement to seek well-being often follows the move-ment of the resources extracted and exploited, and the capital it generates.[15] Colonialism and migration intersect. Puerto Ricans have been migrating to the United States for over 100 years.[16] The most recent migratory wave of the 2010s — mostly to Florida, Texas, and the greater New

York area—was of young professionals and young families seeking financial stability. One of the main causes for this wave was the revelation that the Puerto Rican government had a $70 billion structural debt with U.S. investors. This structural debt also revealed the colonial nature of the Puerto Rico–United States relationship. The Puerto Rico Oversight, Management, and Economic Stability Act (PROMESA) of 2016 established an oversight board appointed by the president of the United States to scrutinize and override any financial legislative action of the government of Puerto Rico that would go against the interest of U.S. vulture investments. The economic and political instability that has ensued due to PROMESA is only exacerbated by the devastation caused by Hurricanes Irma and Maria in 2017 and earthquakes that have been shocking the island since January 2018. Researchers at Hunter College estimate that within a year of Maria, 160,000 Puerto Ricans migrated to the United States.[17] Puerto Rico's population is a little over three million. Puerto Rico might be considered atypical because of its colonial relationship with the United States. However, the metanarrative that enables unfettered intervention by the United States in Puerto Rican affairs is the same one that has encouraged U.S. intervention in Central America. The long history of raw material extraction, land appropriation for single-crop farming, training of local military personnel in U.S. installations for the service of U.S. economic interests, and the support of right-wing dictatorships are all expressions of U.S. colonial enterprises.

It should be no wonder that decades of this self-centered behavior continue to cause the mass movement of Central Americans through Mexico to the southern border of the United States. This movement follows the trail of U.S. exploitation and extraction of Central American wealth. This migratory movement is met with migration policies that, predicated on the history of Manifest Destiny, the Monroe Doctrine, and the Doctrine of Discovery, seeks to cause further harm to those seeking life, liberty, and some ability to pursue happiness. The separation of children from their adult companions at the border is both criminal and culturally American. This is not the first time the United States has instilled terror in those marginalized by white supremacy. And this will not be the last time. Only by confronting and dismantling the root of U.S. exceptionalism will Western terrorism and imperialism end. Colonialism is a cause for migration. The ideology that encourages colonialism is the same ideology used to craft the laws that make it difficult, even downright dangerous, for those marginalized by white supremacy to seek their well-being. Colonialism that results in migration, both of them fostered by the ideology of the Doctrine of Discovery, Manifest Destiny, and the Monroe Doctrine, is a global reality.

It is imperative to remember that this ideology is a political agenda that has been intentionally articulated and theologically undergirded by church institutions. This causes a cacophony in our missional and social witness as Christians in the United States. The late nineteenth- and early twentieth-century North American and Western European Protestant missionary endeavors were founded on these theologies and in support of Western economic and political expansion into the "global South." The cacophony in the U.S. Christian witness is deep and wide. The presence in our midst of people who come from these intentionally marginalized and exploited communities can be seen as a thorn on the side of the U.S. Christian way of life.

The presence of those marginalized and exploited by the actions of our churches can also be seen as invitations to decolonize the narrative and to reconsider what and how it is that we have come to understand the "normal" way of being the church. It is an invitation to center the understanding of what loving Jesus and his message means in yearning for liberation, dignity, welcome, justice, and peace.[18] This invitation is also to grapple with the U.S. Christian use of colonialist tactics in our missionary endeavors of the last century. Christian denominations would intentionally divide the regions they went to evangelize, often making only one way of living the faith (with its biblical interpretation, theology, and liturgy) available. It is not random that the Eastern Baptist Convention of Cuba has a deeper connection to the Southern Baptist Convention, while the Western Baptist Convention of Cuba has a history with the American Baptist Churches USA (the successor body to the Northern Baptist Convention). It is no coincidence that the stronger presence of Puerto Rico Presbyterians is in the western quarter of the island, while Congregationalists have a stronger foothold on the eastern coast. The expansion of Anglicanism throughout the world went mostly hand in hand with the expansion of British imperial and economic influence, while the Presbyterian and Baptist missionary endeavors went hand in hand with U.S. military and economic expansion throughout the world.

These tactics supported and encouraged the ideals of the invasion and expansion. Every incursion of U.S. Christian missionary work that came at the heels of the imposition of U.S. interests in any region was also an endeavor to Americanize.[19] Americanization was the policy in which the church readily participated against Native Americans, enslaved Africans, persons in conquered territories after the Spanish-American War, and groups of immigrants from nonwhite, non-Western, non-Protestant countries. We are challenged to pay attention to the stories of how the marginalized came to know Jesus and also the conflict they bear (political and cultural) of having learned about the witness of Jesus through acts of military intervention, political invasion of homelands, and exploitation of resources often considered sacred by indigenous cultures. We are invited to have the conversation about what it means to be serving in a church that still seeks to fragment the discussion about the repercussion of white supremacy in the church's mission and the social being for its own comfort. Those who serve the U.S. church and come from a group that is marginalized by the country's policies and the church's complicity and participation in those policies are called to serve but conflicted at the same time. Will you listen to their stories and learn from them? Will you join in the work of dismantling white supremacy and the church's participation in it?

CHAPTER 7

POLICE BRUTALITY AND BLACK LIVES MATTER

In front of me stands an army of police officers wearing full body armor and carrying bulletproof shields. Behind me, a Black mother, her throat raw from chanting and with tears streaming down her face, yells, "It's the little things. It's the constant pulling us over for stupid shit or for no reason at all. It's the way you call our men 'Boy' and pull their pants down in the middle of the streets. It's all of the little things you do to intimidate us, to scare us—that's why we're here!" When her throat clogs with a sob, a young Black man wearing baggy jeans and impressively clean white shoes continued, "Nah, it's not just little stuff. Y'all slam us on the ground and pull us out of our cars when we ain't done nothin'. You kick us, beat us, and tase us. And y'all don't hesitate to kill us! Man, fuck the police!"

I flinched when the young man cursed at the police. This was in 2015, on my first night serving in the Black Lives Matter movement as a protest chaplain on the streets of Ferguson, Missouri. I flinched because my relationship to police simply didn't sync with that of the protestors. I just didn't understand their complaints. More honestly, I'm not sure that I even really believed them.

My disbelief of the protestors in Ferguson was due in part to my previous occupation. Before becoming an ordained Episcopal priest, I served as an EMT (emergency medical technician) in Atlanta. As fellow first-responders, police and EMTs are part of the same club. We look out for one another. We respect each other. In fact, a police officer once saved my life by tackling a combative patient who was just inches from hurting me. So in my personal experience, police are helpful and not harmful.

Five years later, after spending countless nights serving on the frontlines of Black Lives Matter protests and truly bearing witness to the testimonies of suffering from protestors, I now understand that both narratives are true: Police *do* abuse some of the very citizens that they swore to protect, *and* they protect other citizens (and property) deemed worthy of protection. A central aim of the Black Lives Matter movement is to address this incongruence in the policing of America.

Police Brutality and Black Lives Matter: A History

"The third degree [by police] that is, the use of physical brutality, or other forms of cruelty, to obtain involuntary confessions or admissions is widespread.
— 1931 Report on Lawlessness in Law Enforcement, Wickersham Commission

The experiences I hear about in 2020 from Black Atlantans at Black Lives Matter protests are remarkably similar to the experiences of others in the 1990s, the 1970s, the 1960s, the 1920s, and every other generation since the creation of slave patrols in the American South during the eighteenth century. Black people, poor people, immigrants, and LGBTQ people have borne the burden of police brutality in both rural and urban neighborhoods across the centuries. Throughout the history of the United States, people's experiences of being beaten, raped, unlawfully detained, harassed, and murdered by police went undocumented and ignored, or complaints were simply dismissed as irrelevant. While marginalized groups in the United States knew of police brutality firsthand, most of white America either turned a blind eye to the abuses, or their gated-off segregated white communities kept police brutality out of their sights. The invention of transportable television cameras helped bring police brutality into view for white Americans and the world.

The architects of the civil rights movement of the 1950s and 1960s strategically made use of the presence of news cameras. But the images of fire hoses, dogs, and police with billy clubs being used on children protesting in Birmingham's Kelly Ingram Park brought the United States to a point of reckoning. This public display of outright police brutality and malice paved the way for an end to public segregation in Alabama and ultimately assisted in the passing of the 1964 Civil Rights Act.

The presence of video cameras continued to play a major role in bringing the issue of police brutality to the fore. In 1991, a personal camcorder captured the violent beating of Rodney King, a Black man, by four Los Angeles police officers. Despite video evidence, none of the officers was convicted of a crime. The people protested.

Oscar Grant, an unarmed, handcuffed Black man was killed by a police officer in 2009 in Oakland, California.

His murder was captured by a bystander on a cell phone. When the officer was sentenced to just two years in prison, the people protested.

Police forces across the nation have installed cameras on the dashboards of police cars, and many law enforcement agencies have even put body cameras on police officers' uniforms. These efforts are designed to help increase police accountability. Despite this heightened level of surveillance, the brutality continues.

The Black Lives Matter movement was birthed in February 2013 when a civilian named George Zimmerman was not convicted for the murder of a teenager named Trayvon Martin in Sanford, Florida. Even though this murder was not an act of police brutality, the non-conviction was a blatant reminder of the ways that the criminal justice system in the United States continuously fails to deliver justice when Black people experience brutalization.

The value of Black lives is the core tenet of the Black Lives Matter movement because underscoring the inherent worth of Black people stands in direct contradiction to the supremacist ideologies upon which the United States is founded. The Black Lives Matter movement dismantles the supremacist notion that some citizens are more worthy of protection than others. The movement refuses to accept a continued reality in which some people's children are more worthy of returning home after an encounter with the police than are other people's children.

The movement picked up more energy when, in 2014, a dashcam captured footage of the murder of Tamir Rice in Cleveland, Ohio. Tamir was a twelve-year-old Black boy playing in a park with a toy gun. The white officer shot Tamir immediately upon arriving on the scene. The officer was not indicted. The people protested.

When Michael Brown, an unarmed Black teenager

was gunned down in Ferguson, Missouri, Black Lives Matter became a worldwide movement. That summer of 2014, people across the world protested against police brutality by taking over highways and sitting in shopping malls. The protest picked up even more steam that November when the officer who killed Brown was not indicted. In fact, a regular chant used at Black Lives Matter rallies includes a long and growing list of Black people's names — all killed by the police — followed by the words "no conviction."

On May 25, 2020, a teenage girl used her cell phone to film a police officer kneeling on the neck of a handcuffed Black man for eight minutes and forty-six seconds. Less than twenty-four hours later millions of people around the world watched the video of George Floyd crying out for mercy as the officer callously suffocated him to death. In response to this public witness of police brutality, George Floyd's name and image became a symbol and rallying cry for the Black Lives Matter movement. The people protested. And as of this writing, 159 days after Floyd's death, the people are *still* protesting.

Like movements for Black lives in previous generations, the Black Lives Matter movement insists that we awaken to the issues of broken policing in America. Through tactics such as blocking major highways and shutting down entire shopping centers, the Black Lives Matter movement forces those in power to stop conducting business as usual and to instead hear the cries of an oppressed people. To help dismantle the false belief that the problem is with how citizens behave during police encounters (the idea that the person who was beaten or killed by police must have done something wrong), protestors chant, "Hands up! Don't shoot!" People wear T-shirts that read, "I am Breonna Taylor" and "I am George Floyd," as a reminder of our shared humanity with those who are victimized.

How Does This Happen?

How is it possible that in a nation now decades past the civil rights movement, Black people who encounter police, for whatever reason, are three times more likely to end up dead than are white Americans?[1] (It's critical to remember here how often Black people are confronted by police for reasons that come nowhere near breaking the law.) Several factors offer at least a partial response to this question.

First, police officers hold significant discretionary power. This is partly because the Supreme Court has conferred this power upon them in increasing measure over the last four decades. Michelle Alexander's book *The New Jim Crow* provides a stunning analysis of a series of cases in which citizens tried to hold police officers accountable for racially biased profiling. The court repeatedly ruled that the only way to prove racially discriminatory practice and policy—and thus the only way to stop a practice for being unconstitutional—was to prove racist intent.[2] Few will openly admit to intending racism; thus, this is an impossibly high legal bar that has allowed racist behavior to continue to run rampant.

Another layer of discretion has to do with the social power conferred on police. Anyone who has been pulled over for speeding is likely to know the nervous feeling that can result. Imagine an officer behaving in a rude or aggressive manner during such a stop. All else being equal (no racial, age, or gender difference), it takes a high level of confidence and courage to challenge such treatment in this most mundane level of encounter. Combine this ethos with the reality that most complaints pit an officer's word against a civilian's, and one can easily see that power functions to give police a great deal of leeway in terms of how they treat people.

Police officers may be no more likely to abuse power in the face of such discretion than any nonuniformed civilian might be. However, they do not need to be more likely to do so in order for such discretion to create a policing crisis. The shocking evidence revealed about human behavior in the infamous Stanford experiment suggests that many people will abuse power if given the opportunity. When two groups of people were set up randomly to be prison guards and prisoners during this 1971 experiment, within a few days the guards—seemingly average, normal people— became so brutal in their treatment of the prisoners that the experiment had to be halted.[3] The experiment strongly indicates that any of us are at risk of abusing power. When those in such a position have weapons and are backed by a system that has repeatedly shown it will confer the benefit of the doubt on them, it is no surprise we have a crisis.

An added layer to the crisis is the persistence of racial bias. Alexander cites a study that demonstrates the extent to which antiBlack racial bias is a pervasive and normal part of Americans' attitudes even among those who disavow racist beliefs. Racism is in the air as a result of U.S. history, social organization, images in media, and a host of other factors. Most of us do not even realize the extent to which we harbor biases.[4] Social psychology is increasingly finding that our racial socialization is so deep that work to undo these biases through strategies such as diversity trainings and multicultural appreciation is extremely limited in its efficacy unless it is rigorous, consistent, and ongoing.[5]

Meanwhile, as with discretionary power, there is no reason to expect a police officer to be any less likely to be shaped by, and thus act out of, racial bias. Saying so is not a defense of brutality. It is an honest recognition of the depth of the problem and another argument for seeing such violence as systemic and, thus, requiring unrelenting and multidirected responses. Anything less becomes a willingness to tolerate police violence against communities of color.

Racial Differences Matter

The depth of racial separation in the United States makes police violence much more difficult to stop. This is because it has been hard to convince the demographic majority of the population (i.e., whites) that there is a problem at all. After Michael Brown was killed, stark racial differences were apparent with everything from whether race was a significant factor in his death to whether the officer should be tried for murder.[6] Eighty percent of Blacks (compared to 18 percent of whites) said that the killing "raises important issues about race that merit discussion."[7]

White people know very little about the day-to-day experience of Black people because most white people know almost no Black people in a meaningful way. A 2013 poll indicated that most white Americans have a social network that is 91 percent white. Three-quarters reported that "the network of people with whom they discuss important matters is entirely white."[8] This level of racial separation makes it difficult for whites to accept what they hear their fellow citizens saying about police violence. Meanwhile, if one has never been stopped because of one's skin tone and has primarily had positive experiences with police, one is repeatedly confirmed in the false belief that all officers are basically trustworthy and the law is objective and just.

Another racially inflected response exists in public debate over the legitimacy of the "violence" of protestors. Here again, when one expects and experiences a system responsive to oneself, one is more likely to presume "legal" and "legitimate" protests to be the only morally accept-able options. Those whose experience is with a system that has never yet been responsive—as was the case with Rosa Parks—know something very different about what is legit-imate, even required, to even be heard.

The point here is not to slip into a simplistic debate over whether or not violence in protests is legitimate. It is to emphasize that larger systems of racial division ensure that whites are insulated from the realities Black people con-tend with every day. These exacerbate our racial divisions and must be taken into account if we care about justice and wish to respond to police brutality.

A Theological Perspective

To help us think about the crises of policing in America, the Black Lives Matter movement, and how we might respond, let's step away from this modern era and instead look at the biblical character Moses.

The Story of Moses

Moses was born in a time when it was dangerous to be a Hebrew boy. Simply because he was Hebrew, his life was considered expendable and of no value. Indeed, because he was a Hebrew boy in the land of Egypt, his very existence was considered threatening. So in an effort to spare his life, his mother strategically arranged for him to be adopted by those who enslaved her people.

Consequently, Moses grew up with an immense amount of privilege. He sat in the halls of power. He undoubtedly received the best of things: the best education, the best seats in the theater, the best food and clothes. After all, he was a prince of Egypt. But one day, in the midst of all of the finery, Moses saw a taskmaster, an overseer, beating an enslaved person.

Now let's be clear here: Long before this day, Moses heard grumblings about the brutality. There is no doubt that he had heard Hebrew mothers wailing as their sons were beaten. Despite living in a different neighborhood than his Hebrew siblings, Moses knew something about the constant surveillance, forced labor, and brutality that they endured. Perhaps in order to make sense of it, he told himself, "Oh, it can't be that bad." Or when he heard the distinct sounds of lashes, maybe he thought to himself, "That guy must have done something very wrong."

The Bible doesn't tell us what made this day different. But for some reason, for the first time, Moses actually saw the brutality for what it is. When he saw that officer/ taskmaster beating his kin, something shifted inside of Moses. Perhaps he remembered that he too was Hebrew, or maybe he caught a glimpse of the humanity in the tear-filled eyes of the victim? Maybe that young man called out for his momma and triggered something inside of Moses's heart. Again, we don't know exactly what changed, but something awakened inside of Moses.

However, instead of going back to the halls of power in which he lived (remember that his grandfather was the pharaoh) and demanding that those in power do something to stop the oppression, Moses, in an act of rage, simply got rid of the "bad apple." He eliminated the one taskmaster and left the unjust slavocracy completely intact.

The Analysis

The church, like Moses, is slow to respond to issues of police brutality. Just as the walls of Pharaoh's palace insulated Moses, the class and racial segregation of neighborhoods, schools, workplaces, and churches makes it easier for those in more privileged places to simply ignore or dismiss the problems of others. And when the grumblings of racial oppression do make their way into our walled-off communities, people often think that the problem must be with how Black people engage police, instead of thinking about how the entire criminal justice system disenfranchises Black people.

In order to participate in the work of ending police brutality, it is imperative that people, especially white people, *listen to Black people*. Listening to Black people requires that one move beyond the economically and racially segregated spaces that are the norm. Listening requires setting aside one's personal beliefs about police and acknowledging that others have entirely different experiences.

Moses' story provides another point of caution. Once he sees the injustice, Moses feels compelled to act, and to do so immediately. In the midst of his newfound wokeness, Moses strikes out on his own and ultimately does much more harm than good. He attempts to address a systemic problem (slavocracy) with an interpersonal response (killing the taskmaster). We see this paralleled when a white church engages in a pulpit swap with a Black church to address racial unrest in a city.

Instead of striking out on one's own to find a quick solution to police brutality, it is important to take the time to educate oneself further about the issues. This type of education is best done in community. Read liberation theology. Learn more about prison abolitionists and the Black Lives Matter movement, and fill in knowledge gaps about the history of policing in the United States and in your own town. Before you act, learn from Black leaders about historical and current forms of Black resistance to police brutality in your area.

Lastly, Moses failed to leverage his privilege on behalf of others. He was a prince. He had access to the pharaoh and ostensibly to the entire ruling class. Moses walked in the halls of power. But instead of demanding that those in charge change things, he abdicated his power and ran away. This is the work that the Black Lives Matter movement calls each of us to: to leverage our individual and collective power in order to bring about justice for all. Indeed, this is the work of the gospel: to wrestle against the principalities, against the powers, against the rulers of injustice in this world.

CHAPTER 8

<hr>

SOCIAL MEDIA AND THE
U.S. RACIAL DIVIDE

Human beings are social creatures. For followers of Judaism and Christianity, this is evidenced in two stories at the very beginning of the Hebrew Scriptures. The creation stories of Genesis have humans created by a God desiring interaction with God's creation. Humans are modeled off of a social God; this is hinted in the statement "Let *us* create humankind in *our* image," where God is not a solitary entity but the epitome of interaction and relationship. Humans are then encouraged to multiply and steward the earth, which requires social interaction. The second creation story of Genesis has God concerned about the loneliness of the first human. God then creates another human, thereby forming the bonds of relationship and the need to be social with God and with each other. Those social bonds are further described by God's word, "Thereby a human leaves their parent and clings to their own partner."

Even the sharing of holy stories and histories are a societal action. The first forms of social media were oral storytelling, with histories and stories passed from generation to generation through spoken word. In order for information to become known to a community, it must be transferred through social channels. The channels have varied throughout the course of human history, from oral storytelling, drawings, the formation of written words, and the printing press. History has also shown that information is power; whoever has the attention of the masses not only can transfer information to those masses, but that information can alter how the masses interpret the world and the communities around them.

The form of information sharing prevalent today is social media. Social media has radically altered how people interact with one another. Individuals are more connected than ever before with others around the world, and the transfer of information is near instantaneous. Because of social media platforms such as Facebook, Twitter, Instagram, and YouTube, people are more immediately connected across the world than at any other time in human history. This connectivity is resulting in the transfer of massive amounts of information around the world in real time. Instead of waiting days and weeks for information to travel via handwritten letters or having to pay exorbitant amounts of money to make a phone call overseas, communication over the internet, especially through social media, has opened the floodgates of communication and accessible information. Because of this low-cost and near-instantaneous way to communicate, diverse populations from around the world have access to this technology to stay connected to the rest of the world.[1]

Weaponized Social Media

Facebook founder and CEO Mark Zuckerberg repeatedly states at public gatherings, "Facebook gives people the power to share in order to make the world more open and connected."[2] Unfortunately, Facebook has been one of the culprits of creating intense racial divides among people. With the floodgates of information open to anyone who has access to social media platforms, nearly anyone can post anything on the internet. Social media has become a frighteningly effective weapon not only to sow discord but also to inflame divisions among people. Misinformation on social media has the power to divide and conquer, including on matters of race in the United States. Information on social media news feeds are driven by algorithms, which means that information is curated and designed for specific users to keep them online for longer amounts of time. Information needs to capture attention; since technology has decreased the human attention span, there is a need to create content that will capture an individual's attention for substantial amounts of time.[3] In social media feeds, that content has become increasingly divisive, which has been fueled by those wanting to maintain power.

Information is power, and misinformation can cause immense amounts of destruction, including the loss of human life. Sources of information have the potential to change opinions. Information deemed as true by one community can be regarded as entirely false by another. How that information is disseminated and interpreted can reveal hidden animosities and grudges, as witnessed in the 2016 presidential election. Information from social media was able not only to change the course of a nation's history and political situation, but it also came with great power to both unite and divide communities.

Leading up to the election in November 2016, it was found that the Russian government was using social media to influence opinions.[4] Russia used Ukraine as a testing ground before unleashing waves of misinformation to the United States leading up to the election. Facebook was a primary culprit, as Facebook was not prepared to address a massive and strategized misinformation campaign taking place within its platform. The misinformation campaign was exacerbated with the reveal of the Cambridge Analytica scandal, where users' personal data was harvested without their consent by Cambridge Analytica, with that data being used for targeted political ads. This breach of information led Mark Zuckerberg to testify in front of Congress. During his testimony, it was revealed that members of Congress had little knowledge about the workings of social media, revealing that it was a perfect tool to sow discord throughout society, including into the highest echelons of U.S. government.

Fake accounts led to fake news, as actors and agents were intentionally spreading misinformation to sow discord and divides within the United States. Such discord and divide fostered already-deep racial divisions within the United States, with far right and white supremacist groups utilizing social media to further their causes. Far right and white supremacist rallies began to take place across the United States, emboldened by the results of the 2016 election. Social media gave these communities the means to connect and to mobilize, as seen in the 2017 Unite the Right Rally in Charlottesville, Virginia, that led to the death of a counterprotestor. Online movements such as 4Chan have increased traffic to their websites, and QAnon has established its ways of information sharing over Twitter and YouTube.

Unity in Social Media

Not all is lost on social media. Social media also has the incredible power to bring people together to organize in efforts toward combating racism. Three queer Black women, Alicia Garza, Patrisse Cullors, and Opal Tometi, were able to use a hashtag to create a global movement. The #BlackLivesMatter movement is the paramount example of using social media to bring people together for a common cause and using hashtag activism to spread information and awareness about the underlying racism in which the United States has always been steeped.

Social media has become a useful tool in coordinating large-scale protests, as witnessed through multiple gatherings across the country to protest racial injustice. Social media has the ability to inform and to organize and mobilize the masses to take to the streets to protest racial injustice. When the Trump administration attempted to enforce its Muslim ban in January 2017, thousands of protestors showed up at airports across the United States within hours. Many people who were finding a way to show their disagreement first took to social media. Some had organized gatherings at airports and sent out invitations to their networks. As more people received information about these gatherings and saw friends responding, more felt compelled to physically show up at airports. Social media can also be used as a safety tool. Protesters can turn to social media and hashtags for real-time information to find out where authorities are gathered and if counterprotests and violence are taking place. Protestors connected on social media experience strength and safety in numbers, and they can coordinate money and arrangements for bail in case arrests occur.

From their computer screens and phones, people who are unable to attend a physical protest not only are able to share information with one another; they are also able to lament and rejoice together in the fight for racial justice. Online communities through hashtags have given people an outlet to express their feelings in fighting racism; some of the communities created through the power of these hashtags have led people to share artistic and creative practices with one another. Despite the critique of "slactivism"—that reposting information isn't active and engaged action to combat racism—sharing information over social media for social justice causes invites people of all abilities to participate in movement work.[5] Sharing stories and experiences with one another is a tool to create bonds within communities, whether they be physical or online.

Organizations rooted in racial justice are turning to online communication as a means to educate the masses with webinars, book offerings, and coaching for those who are committed to a more just and equitable world. Communities such as SURJ (Showing Up for Racial Justice) have harnessed the power of networks to create chapters across the United States, offering a hybrid of online and physical gatherings to share in the work of antiracism.

A Social Church Online

Overall, the institutionalized church has been slow to adopt current ways of communication. While there are a few faith communities that are early adopters of technology, the institutional church usually maintains a status quo, fearing innovation. The institutional church often turns to innovation in communication out of panic over decline rather than proactively as part of its mission. Most manifestations of the church are years, if not decades, behind on ways and forms to communicate with others.

The onset of the COVID-19 pandemic in the United States forced many churches to innovate against their will. In order to remain physically distanced for the health and safety of their members, many churches were forced to turn to social media for worship services and programming. This move from physical meetings in buildings to virtual spaces has shown churches that online forms of connection can be used not only for political purposes but also for faith-based connections.

As churches enter the foray of digital spaces, some are becoming increasingly aware not just of the power of social media but of the great responsibility that accompanies it. Some faith communities have created online spaces to organize around combating racism and misinformation, which has led to increased divisions within the United States. Members of faith communities have brought information from social media, some of it false, into their gathering spaces. Religious leaders have turned to online communities to seek support, information, and advice on how to handle misinformation with their members.

Religious leaders have also utilized social media to express their views outside the physical walls of their communities. Many have become outspoken in virtual spaces in addressing the damage racism causes individually and corporately, and how that damage has also impacted their communities. Their followers are not just members of their respective faith communities, but others as well. Having these robust online conversations has led to a variety of outcomes: disgruntled members, a way to open conversation on difficult topics, and a public forum involving a global audience.

Social media has become an effective way for religious leaders to connect with others, engage with questions, and push back against general assumptions in antiracism work. For religious leaders who frequently post about antiracism work where demographics trend toward white, rural, and impoverished, social media gives such leaders an opportunity not only to publicly state their commitments, but also to connect with those who do not agree with the norms of their area. It is an opportunity to provide visibly progressive leadership where progressivism is not widely appreciated. This leadership gives members of the faith communities and also the wider regional communities a chance to engage in and wrestle with conversations that they would not normally have. Social media posts coming from religious leaders that challenge others to take on antiracism work have empowered members of faith communities to engage in antiracism work and to voice their perspectives, even when those perspectives go against popular opinion in a given community. This provides community members with a different way to advocate for racial justice.

Religious leaders and members of faith communities engage in online spaces because it is an important way to communicate effectively and receive information. Christians must engage their faith in how they communicate with others, whether it be in the flesh or through social media. Followers of Jesus need to recall that there is a need to proclaim the gospel, and that every person encountered must be regarded as created in the image of God, even if that individual is behind a phone or computer screen. Algorithms do not care about the humanity of a person and treat that individual as a product. The algorithms used to gain attention and lengthen screen time do not regard the lived experiences of a person as unique and holy.

Conclusion

Social media forms bonds and connections and is used for both good and ill. It is also drastically changing how we interact with one another. Information is power, and this power has to be acknowledged on a multitude of fronts. Information that is provided over the internet, whether it be true or false, has power in attracting attention. Social media companies hold the power of information when using data shared by individuals through their app usage for financial gain. Companies also increase profits through mining user data to increase the attractiveness of a feed, drawing consumers to it for longer. Many of the algorithms for these platforms use the most controversial content. Oftentimes this controversial content fosters greater racial divisions. Some feed into the controversial content to stoke the fires of racism, while others are using social media to form antiracist communities and practices in an attempt to put the fires out.

Christians are called to hold one another accountable, whether that be in the flesh or over the internet. The words in John's Gospel that the Word was made flesh should remind Christians that the words on computer screens are also words attached to people's flesh. The age of increased social media usage shows that words have power to both give life and to take it away. Social media, especially from a Christian perspective, should be used to bring abundant life to the fullness of God's creation, as opposed to giving in to the power of the principalities and idols of this world that seek to destroy.

CHAPTER 9

⟨⟨⟨∞⟩⟩⟩

DO SEGREGATED
CHURCHES IMPLY RACISM?

In an interview at Western Michigan University in 1963,
Martin Luther King Jr. spoke about segregation in the
church. He was responding to a question about whether
or not he thought integration should occur in the church
before it took place in public venues such as schools,
department stores, and public parks. He said,

> We must face the fact that in America, the church
> is still the most segregated major institution . . . .
> At 11:00 on Sunday morning when we stand and
> sing and Christ has no east or west, we stand at the
> most segregated hour in this nation. This is tragic.
> Nobody of honesty can overlook this. Now, I'm
> sure that if the church had taken a stronger stand all
> along, we wouldn't have many of the problems that
> we have. The first way that the church can repent,
> the first way that it can move out into the arena of
> social reform is to remove the yoke of segregation
> from its own body.[1]

Several points in this statement are helpful in exploring racial segregation in the church. First, King was disappointed with the hypocrisy of the church, which sang about the oneness of Christ in worship yet actively engaged in racial segregation every week and did not take a more active role in challenging the ideology of racism. Second, he believed that the church played a role in the proliferation of segregation. Third, he believed that the church should repent of its sins by ceasing to practice racial segregation in worship.

Was King correct about the church helping to proliferate racism? Is it in the best interest of all concerned for the church to become integrated? What does true integration look like? Before we can respond to these questions, it is important to understand a bit more about the impetus of racial ideology and the history of racial segregation in churches in the United States.

Origin of Racial Ideology

The United States of America was founded on the principles of equality, civil rights, democracy, justice, and freedom for all people. As a result, the only way the colonies could justify the enslavement of Black people was to depict them as less than human. Physical characteristics such as skin color, nose width, eye shape, and hair texture became markers of racial identity. When Chinese and Japanese people came into the country in the nineteenth century, they were integrated into the status continuum somewhere between Black people and European whites. Along with privileging by racial identity came cultural hegemony, in which European culture was privileged above all other cultures. Africans and other racial groups were taught to have disdain for their native cultures and to revere European culture in all things. One area in which the influence of European cultural hegemony can be evidenced even today is education. European literature, history, music, and visual arts are often still the standards against which all other cultural contributions are measured.

In order to understand the particulars of the ideology of race, one has only to read *Notes on the State of Virginia* by Thomas Jefferson. In his book, Jefferson writes a blueprint for racial stereotyping of Black people that exists to this day.[2] According to Jefferson, the inferiority of Black people starts with the color of their skin, which is the foundation of a "greater or less share of beauty." Whites have "flowing hair and more elegant symmetry of form." Jefferson not only contends that Black people are inferior in color, figure, and hair, but that they have a "very strong and disagreeable odor." Even the love Black people display toward one another is inferior to that shared by whites, since Black men are more prone to "desire" than "tender delicate mixture of sentiment and sensation." Black people are "much inferior" to whites in reason, participating more in "sensation than reflection." Jefferson admits that Black people are more gifted than whites in music, having an "accurate ear for tune and time." However, he is not convinced that Black people can equal whites in their ability to compose "extensive melodies" or "complicated harmony." At the end of the "Laws" section of his book, Jefferson writes that the differences of "mental faculty and color" are "powerful obstacles to emancipation" of Black people.

Brief History of Racially Segregated Worship

The ideology of race was not limited to the public square but was manifest in Christian worship. Though Africans worshiped in the same churches, they were often relegated to separate areas. One example is St. George's Methodist Church in Philadelphia in the eighteenth century. Though many white Methodists of that day objected to the practice of slavery, they did not believe that Africans were their equals.[3] As a result, the white members of St. George's built a gallery addition to the church and mandated that Africans worship there. Africans also felt stifled in their ability to express themselves in worship with verbal "Amens" or holy dancing. Since he and other Black people were being oppressed and discriminated against, Richard Allen, a newly manumitted African slave, left St. George's and started the African Methodist Episcopal Church. The founding of this new denomination was part of the Black independent church movement that began as an expression of Black resistance to white oppression after the Revolutionary War.[4] During this movement, many Black Baptist churches were founded, as were new Black denominations such as the African Methodist Episcopal Zion Church and the Colored Methodist Episcopal Church (now known as the Christian Methodist Episcopal Church).

The founding of Black mainline Protestant churches was just the beginning of the Black church movement. It began with Black people leaving white Baptist and Methodist churches because of racism. Then some Black people left the Black Baptist and Black Methodist denominations because of a commitment to holiness.[5] In addition to a commitment to holiness, says Cheryl Sanders, the churches were countercultural in the sense that while Black people in the Baptist and Methodist churches "assimilated and imitated the cultural and organizational models of European-American patriarchy," including styles of worship, the sanctified churches allowed Black people to retain the traditions of oral music and ecstatic praise associated with slave religion.[6]

The separation of Black people and whites in Christian worship established a pattern of segregated worship that endures to this day.[7]

The Case for Segregated Worship

Martin Luther King Jr. argued that the church should cease its practice of segregated worship as a first step in its effort to achieve social reform. He made this statement even in the wake of tremendous social gains made by Black people during the civil rights movement wherein Black churches played a vital role. In Black churches, civil rights workers heard prophetic and charismatic preaching that stirred their souls, comforted their spirits, and identified with the daily struggles they encountered. In those Black churches, Black people did not have to censor their speech to be politically correct or sensitive to the feelings of their white sisters and brothers. Black churches were spaces outside of their homes where they not only could speak their minds but where they also could hear messages of renewal to help them cope with the harsh realities of their lives throughout the coming week.

Many Black people learn to appreciate Black history in Black churches, where they are taught about contributions to American history made by people such as Sojourner Truth, Mary McLeod Bethune, Marian Anderson, Frederick Douglass, Charles Drew, and Benjamin Banneker. Learning about other Black people who were accomplished in so many ways inspires young people to make their own contributions.

Even in the twenty-first century, Black churches are usually spaces where Black people can be uncensored. They can hear sermons conceived with Black life experiences in mind. They can hear music presented in genres that meet their spiritual needs. They can pray in ways they inherited from ancestors. They can be free to worship as long as they want. They can worship in an environment that is culturally affirming. They can be assured that their children will learn about their own Black history in Sunday school or worship. As it relates to race, they can be accepted for who they are.

The Case for Truly Integrated Worship

Though the benefits of segregated worship are many, there are also benefits of integrated worship. Truly integrated worship is worship in which the many cultural practices of all races and ethnicities are valued and given space in the worship and life of the community.

Often worship that is deemed *multicultural* is simply an expression of dominant-culture hegemony in which the presence of people of various ethnicities and races is encouraged without allowing their cultural practices, traditions, and values (such as music, liturgy, and preaching styles) to have a place in worship and community life. Churches that practice dominant-culture hegemony expect all members to conform to the ethos of the dominant culture, rather than allowing the dominant culture to be changed by the incorporation of other ways of being. Dominant-culture hegemony is akin to the melting-pot metaphor in which all ingredients are welcome but are expected to surrender their distinctiveness to assume the flavor and texture of the soup.[8] Truly integrated worship is akin to a salad in which all the ingredients blend to create wonderful flavors while each ingredient maintains its own distinctive taste, texture, and color.

Is it possible for a church to be truly integrated? Jin S. Kim, pastor of the Church of All Nations, a congregation of the Presbyterian Church (U.S.A.) in Minneapolis, not only believes it is possible but works with his congregation daily to make it a reality. In 2004, Kim, along with one hundred mostly Korean Americans, was granted a formal blessing by a larger congregation to found the Church of All Nations. The goal was to create a church wherein people from many different races and ethnic groups could come together as the body of Christ. Of the 350 people who attend worship currently, 30 percent are Asian, 37 percent are white, 22 percent are Black, and 10 percent are Latino/a. The congregation is truly living into its name by having people from more than twenty-five different nations represented, including Korea, Kenya, Sudan, Brazil, Japan, and the United States.

Elements of many different cultures are integrated into the English worship service held on Sundays at 10 a.m. Prayers are offered in many different languages. The Glorybound choir offers an extensive repertoire of songs and hymns that reflect the diversity of cultures. Fifty-six flags are displayed in the sanctuary to represent members' countries of origin, with which the congregation is in partnership or in prayer. Testimony, a practice borrowed from the Black tradition in which individuals share their personal joys and struggles with the entire body, is a regular part of worship. Testimonies are sometimes given at offering time. On occasion, testimony replaces the sermon. At least twice a year, the entire service is devoted to testimony. While revealing personal experiences can be very risky, it can also serve as a conduit to understanding. When people hear each other's stories, they may begin to understand and experience the other in new ways.

On Sundays there is a Brazilian service conducted in Portuguese and a Sudanese service conducted in the Nuer language, as well as a service in French attended largely by West Africans; all attendees are full members of the

Church of All Nations. Each of these services has its own musical group. Though Kim would eventually like for the community to worship together in one service regularly (it does so now occasionally), he realizes that offering services in native languages brings tremendous comfort and a sense of belonging to new immigrants in the congregation. The leadership of the church reflects the diversity of the congregation, with pastors from Kenya, Togo, Brazil, China, Sudan, and the United States. With all the diversity that exists in the congregation, Kim contends that the greatest challenge is the Black-white divide. In addition to being truly integrated as it relates to race and ethnicity, the church also dares to be counterimperial in that it rejects the capitalistic emphasis on production and material wealth as the symbols of identity, status, and success. At the Church of All Nations, the people who are held in highest esteem are those whose lives reflect faithfulness to God and care for one another.

Kim believes that the church thrives because its members are willing to engage in hard conversations about white privilege and racism. They openly confess their complicity to unjust structures. Kim realizes that since he is Korean, it would be easy for the Korean culture to be the dominant culture. It would also be easy for white culture to be the dominant culture, since many people in the congregation are indoctrinated in it. However, Kim is intentional about reducing the influence of Korean and white cultures whenever possible to allow space for the many other cultures that exist. His congregation trusts him to be the "cultural referee."

Another congregation that embraces the salad metaphor is the Plymouth United Church of Christ in Oakland, California — also known as the "Jazz and Justice Church." This congregation is 59 percent Euro-American, 31 percent Black, 5 percent Asian, and 5 percent Latino. The jazz part of its identity is a metaphor in the sense that worship is a practice of living in the moment—an experience in which improvisation is welcome and there is no such thing as a mistake. Jazz is also experiential. Musicians from the Bay Area, many of whom are Black, provide music for the worship service throughout the year, which helps to create a lively and soulful worship environment. Though jazz is a large part of the church's identity, gospel music and hymns are also part of the musical repertoire.

Like the Church of All Nations, Plymouth UCC makes time in its worship service for testimony with a weekly spot known as "grace notes." The congregation strives to have open and honest discussions about racism, sexism, and ageism. As it relates to staff, they discovered a possible correlation between diversification of ministry staff and diversification of the congregation. For example, when a gay minister was hired, other lesbian, gay, bisexual, and transgendered (LGBT) people started to attend services. When a Cuban American minister was hired, other Latinos/as began attending worship. The artwork in the church is African, Asian, or Latin American in origin; the church is intentional about not having white images of Jesus displayed. In addition, the church celebrates cultural festivals and holidays such as Juneteenth and Cinco de Mayo.

Conclusion

In response to the question "Do segregated churches imply racism?" we must respond with a resounding yes. The impetus for the establishment of segregated churches was racism embodied in censorship and the relegation of Black people to separate spaces in white churches. Some believe that the antidote to the traditional segregated church is the melting-pot church, in which many different races and ethnicities are represented in body but are not represented in the leadership and must see their cultural practices and traditions subsumed into the dominant culture. This model is disingenuous at best. The real antidote to traditional segregated worship is the salad church. In the salad model, ethnic and racial groups are not required to deny or abdicate who they are to be part of the community. Their practices and traditions are welcomed and integrated into all aspects of worship and community life.

The perpetuation of segregated churches implies the ongoing need of various racial and ethnic groups to have spaces in which they can freely and unashamedly worship without fear of judgment or disdain — places where they can have a sense of pride and solidarity with people who look like them and who have similar values and shared experiences. Even in the twenty-first century, many racial and ethnic groups still have few public spaces in which their cultural practices and traditions are honored, respected, and embraced.

Therefore, the task for any church that seeks to be truly integrated is for church leaders to be willing to relinquish their power and then take it up again. The power that is relinquished is the *absolute* power that maintains an exclusive and discriminatory congregational ethos. The power taken up is a *shared* power that invites all people to the table, embraces who they are, and invites them to share their whole selves with the community. Shared power enables the church to become more like what it is meant to be: the body of Christ.

PART III

WHAT TO DO

CHAPTER 10

WHITENESS AND WHAT
WHITE PEOPLE CAN DO

Many contemporary white people rightly argue that *we** did not commit genocide against native peoples in this country. *We* didn't enslave Black people. *We* didn't fight in the war that stole half of Mexico and that is now the western United States. *We* weren't even alive when the Chinese Exclusion Act happened, and *we* didn't intern Japanese citizens during World War II. Those things happened decades or even centuries ago. So why should we white people today bear any responsibility for something that *we* didn't do?

The simple answer is that white people continue to benefit from a system that was built and still operates to give us an unfair advantage and others an unfair disadvantage. It is true that many white people are struggling to make

---

*This chapter is written by white people to other white people specifically. For that reason, "we" refers to white people. Others certainly are encouraged to read this and participate in the discussion.

ends meet and don't feel very privileged when credit cards are maxed out and budgets are stretched to the limit. Nevertheless, if we think *we* have it bad, others have it much worse. And if we truly believe that all children of God are equal, we need to act when some are not treated as equally as others.

One sign of white advantage or white privilege is that we don't actually *have* to do anything. It is tempting to shrug our shoulders and excuse our inaction on a lack of political leadership, the complexity of the issues, and mixed messages about just what to do. This chapter explains whiteness as a concept that arose in order to separate and give privilege to one group of people, explains what white privilege is with some examples, and offers some ideas about how to help dismantle racism.

The Origins of Whiteness in America

In the book *Dear White Christians*, Jennifer Harvey explains the history of whiteness as a racial category in the United States and how it arose as an identity simultaneous with and related to the "violent and complete subjugation of the darker skinned."[1] The following is a simplified summary of how race first emerged in the United States.

Despite the popular narrative about America's founders coming to escape religious persecution, Christopher Columbus sailed the ocean blue in 1492 looking for treasure. Most Europeans who settled in the Virginia area were English elites coming to pursue wealth. Tobacco was the most lucrative crop, and it required large numbers of workers to produce. While the primary source of labor was originally tenant farmers from Europe, this quickly transformed to an indentured servant system, which was more profitable for the colonial elites. Harvey points out that, hard as indentured servanthood was, it never approached the level and cruelty of chattel slavery.[2]

The first documentation of an African servant in America was in 1619. There is not much written about the period from 1619 to 1640, but a court case in 1640 changed everything. Three indentured servants escaped from their owner and were caught. One was a Dutchman, one a Scotchman, and one a person of African descent. The two Europeans were given whippings and sentenced to additional time as servants. But the African, also whipped, was sentenced to return and to serve his master for life. No European servant ever received this sort of life sentence.

Harvey observes that the other notable element in the case was that for the first time, "physical difference was invoked specifically and clearly as a means to assign a radically different servitude status to an African person vis-à-vis his European counterparts."[3] The African was called a "Negro" in the court case, referring to his dark skin color (*negro* in Spanish means "dark" or "black").

At the same time, the term used by the English to refer to themselves had evolved from "Christian" (separating themselves from "savage" native peoples and "heathen" Africans) to "English" and "free." But by the end of the century, with the ongoing, brutal genocide of Native Americans and the system of chattel slavery for forcibly relocated Africans, a new term emerged for the elite: white.

This short history explains what people mean when they say that race is a social construct. It was created by people in power based on physical traits such as skin color, hair texture, and eye color to lump people from different ethnic cultures into a group in order to control them.

Not surprisingly, over the next centuries, other lighter-skinned people coming to the United States were willing to participate in this system based on skin color in order to reap the benefits that came with compliance. So just as native peoples from dozens of different ethnic groups and languages were lumped together as *Indians* in this white supremacy model, so darker-skinned Africans from many different ethnic groups and languages were bunched together as *Negro* slaves. And lighter-skinned peoples lost their particular ethnic identities for the most part in exchange for becoming *white*. Is it any wonder that most white people wonder what their heritage is? We may be proud that our great-grandparents were German or Italian and spoke their native languages at home. Yet we also know that if they were light skinned, they (or their children) soon relinquished many of their ethnic customs in order to pass for white and enjoy the privileges that came with that status. Is it any wonder that, while not knowing the entire racist history of the country, most white people feel uncomfortable talking about racism? This feeling is often called *white shame*. Harvey writes:

> Although a majority of whites on this land base were not slaveholders themselves, all occupied Native land, and most refused to disrupt the institution of slavery. Even those whose economic interests were harmed by the existence of slavery benefited from it in various ways. Moreover, slavery could not have functioned were not most whites — rich or poor, third generation or new immigrant — willing to allow it to continue. As long as the system could rely on light-skinned people to choose not to be a safe haven when African peoples ran away, and to choose to serve as overseers, to mill the cotton that moved from South to North, to rely on wages earned in that production to feed their families, and on a myriad of other similar behaviors that ensured slavery functioned, it did not matter that most whites did not themselves own slaves.[4]

Of course, native peoples and forcibly relocated Africans were not the only ones to suffer under this system based on skin color. All people in the country who could not fit under the white umbrella experienced discrimination. And resistance and rebellion have been a constant reaction by darker-skinned peoples and are part of our national history, though absent from many school history textbooks. In addition, many white people, including many Christians, have given their lives in the struggle against a racist system based on inequality and violence.

White Supremacy Continued

Most people passing for white through the nation's history have not consciously participated in this white supremacist system built on the backs of the forced and underpaid labor of darker-skinned peoples. Yet the inequalities did not end with the Civil War or even the Civil Rights Act of 1964, the Voting Rights Act of 1965, and the Fair Housing Act of 1968. The common narrative is that the Civil War ended slavery in the South. Yet we know that is not true. Policies were continually enacted by white political leaders that kept nonwhites poor and with fewer resources. The following is just one example:

> What the federal government did, starting in the 1930s, was demolish many of these integrated neighborhoods and build segregated public housing, separate projects for blacks and separate projects for whites so it created segregation where none had existed before. The second major policy was the federal housing administration, starting in the late 1930s, began to insure loans to mass production builders to build subdivision suburbs around

the country so that whites could move from urban areas to the suburbs and the federal housing administration guaranteed these loans to mass production builders on the explicit condition that no homes be sold to African Americans.[5]

But what we really haven't dealt with is the massive investments that went into creating segregated housing. And unlike other forms of discrimination, when you engage in investments that change the landscape and infrastructure, you cannot undo that simply by ceasing to do that which you did before. . . . So if you have massively invested in the creation of white suburbs through the interstate highway system and through providing the kinds of loans and tax breaks to the creation of all white suburbs, you cannot undo the damage of that simply by no longer making those investments.[6]

White Privilege Today

The term *white privilege* is used to refer to the unearned advantages enjoyed by white people in the United States. Perhaps these privileges are not as visible as they once were. One does not walk past slave pens and watch forcibly removed Africans being sold to white masters. We don't have separate drinking fountains for whites. Yet whether we feel privileged or not, those of us who are white still benefit from the present social order. And as a growing movement is pointing out, racial injustices are visible if we only pay attention. For example, the increased instances (or the increased attention and visibility) of police shootings of innocent Black men and children are evidence of an institution that historically protected white supremacist interests and was never reformed.

Examples of White Privilege

Whites can move into an apartment or house wherever they want and assume that their neighbors will be friendly, oblivious, or unconcerned.

Whites can walk into any store and not fear being followed by security guards or watched.

Whites can dress like slobs and not feel judged for having attire that shows they are obviously poor or lazy. On dress-down Friday, they can really dress down.

Whites aren't afraid of the police. They consider them their friends. Likewise, whites can call 9-1-1 about a fire or for an ambulance and trust that help will come immediately.

Whites can contact any doctor, lawyer, electrician, or plumber and assume they will be treated well.

Whites can check into any hotel and not worry about being told there is no vacancy or being placed in a substandard room while being charged the highest price.

Whites may be alarmed when pulled over for a traffic violation, but they assume they will just get a ticket and not be harassed, searched, or arrested.

If they receive bad service at a business, whites can confront the clerk and insist on seeing the manager while not fearing harassment by the manager or arrest.

If white people fail, their race or moral character is not questioned.

A group of white men armed with assault rifles and other guns can walk into a multiracial crowd of angry protestors and not be shot by police.

Many white folk would prefer to ignore or deny this reality; this is one of the reasons that racism is often defined in terms of personal prejudice. It is easier to think of racism and the tensions and inequality around issues of race as a particular kind of prejudice. That allows certain white people to say that since we are not prejudiced, we don't need to worry about racism or concern ourselves with working toward dismantling it.

Yet racism is a system, not a prejudice. White people and people of color—Black people, Latinos/as, Asian Americans, Native Americans—have very different experiences in the United States because of this system of privilege based on skin color. This may make white people feel uncomfortable, but it is a fact.

Every year, the National Urban League publishes the Equality Index, which compares the conditions of Black, Latino/a, and white Americans using a comprehensive set of variables, including health, education, economics, social justice, and civic engagement. The beginning point is a line from the original Constitution of the United States that counted Black people as three-fifths of a person for purposes of taxation and state representation—or 0.60, using whites as the standard 1.0. (The Constitution was corrected by the Thirteenth Amendment in 1865.) When the index is lower than 1.0, it indicates that Black or Latino Americans are not doing as well as whites in the area being measured. For 2015, the index was 0.72 for Black people and 0.78 for Latinos, essentially unchanged from previous years.[7]

There is a wealth of information in this index. For example, Black Americans are at 0.80 and Latinos are at 1.07 relative to white Americans with regard to health. These numbers have improved greatly in the short time since the Affordable Care Act (i.e., Obamacare) was enacted. Yet in the economic category, the index stands at 0.56 for Black people and 0.61 for Latinos.

In *The Hidden Cost of Being Black*, Thomas Shapiro explains that the true disparity in economic well-being between Black and white Americans is not found primarily in the fact that the average Black family earns sixty-four cents for every dollar earned by the average white family. Rather, it has to do with the way that wealth is passed from generation to generation; the net worth of the average white family is $81,000, compared to $8,000 for the average Black family. The traditional argument is that the difference in wealth has to do with disparities in education, job, and income, but when middle-class families with equivalent education, jobs, and incomes are compared, the average Black family still owns only twenty-six cents for every dollar owned by its white counterpart.[8]

In a system that gives unfair economic advantages to whites, it is difficult for people of color to build wealth. One argument for reparations for people harmed by this system is to help them catch up and to enable them to help future generations succeed. For example, one of the harshest, long-term outcomes of the 1921 Tulsa race massacre—in which whites destroyed a large business and housing community of middle-class, prosperous Black people and murdered over 300 innocent men, women, and children—was the destruction of accumulated wealth that was slowly being passed from one generation to the next, allowing children to attend college and move up the economic ladder. Reparations were never granted. In fact, the Oklahoma legislature passed a law the year following the massacre (still called a "riot" by most of the media) that no reparations could ever be requested. In September 2015, some ninety-five years after the fact, the Tulsa police chief issued an apology for the failure to protect Black people. Yet demands for reparations in the form of college tuition and loan assistance are still denied, making the confession rather empty.

Whiteness and Youth Today

For a 2015 MTV documentary *White People*, Pulitzer Prize–winning journalist and filmmaker Jose Antonio Vargas led some uncomfortable discussions with a diverse group of young adults from across the country about whiteness.[9] He encouraged them to be brutally honest. One of the first questions he asked was "What is white?" Answers included "It's the default," "It's the norm," It's the good thing." When he asked how white people felt about talking with people of another race, answers included "I feel totally comfortable" and "I could care less about someone's race; I was never taught to notice it." Almost all young white Americans he interviewed considered themselves color-blind. He reported that three out of four young white Americans said that society would be better off if we never acknowledged race. Four out of five young white Americans said they feel uncomfortable discussing race issues. Yet others, especially people of color, said that having this point of view was dismissive of people of color. To not acknowledge racism experienced by nonwhite people ignores the reality in which they live. Most white kids reported never talking about racism with their parents. If we think racism will disappear naturally with future generations, this documentary exposes the error of our thinking. White people need to understand how racism works, and they need to work to end it. It will not end by itself, as recent events in our country attest.

What to Do About White Privilege

Our country has never had a conversation about what to do with such a large group of people who have been forcefully placed at the margins and how to help them. A *New*

Yorker article about the 2015 killing of nine Black church members by a young white racist paraphrased Joseph Darby, former pastor of Morris Brown African Methodist Episcopal Church in Charleston, South Carolina: "All the 'kumbaya stuff' will be meaningless without combating the institutional racism that still defines the state 'and the state of the union': underfunded, segregated schools, neglected Black towns, unjust voter I.D. laws, gentrification and joblessness in the cities, outsized rates of African-Americans in prison."[10]

Of course, when we talk about racism in this country, we are not only talking about whites and Black people, as Robette Ann Dias explains:

> If we only understand race as being Black or White, and we only have a framework for understanding racism as dynamics between Black people and White people, defining the "race problem" as the legacy caused by African enslavement, then the solutions we can imagine are constrained to rectifying that dynamic. In the real world, this means we could solve the problem of civil rights, full inclusion, and control of resources for African-Americans, we could even make reparations but still not have touched American Indian's [*sic*] racial justice struggle to reclaim land and sovereignty. Nor would we have solved any issues around immigration and civil rights for people from (or whose ancestors were from) parts of the world that the US restricts legal immigration like Latin and South America, Africa, Asia and the Middle East. The homelands of Puerto Rico, Hawai'i, Alaska, and Guam would still not be returned to their people. And our economy would continue to depend on neo-colonial practices around the world.[11]

Unfortunately, in a racist society where skin color makes such a difference, one cannot simply opt out. People of color certainly cannot ignore the rules of the system. White people can ignore their advantage, but it undeniably exists. Ignoring privilege is itself a sign of privilege.

One natural response of white people is to feel shame. If you are white and someone were to ask you what makes you most proud about your race, you probably would feel uneasy. At a gut level, we know something is wrong and don't really know what it means to be white. We watch white racists with horror as they claim superiority for whiteness. We know that's wrong, but just who are we? Feeling some shame for participating in a system we didn't create but that privileges us is healthy to a degree. Yet we cannot be immobilized by this shame. Instead, we can recognize it and work to dismantle the system.

Another common response to deal with our uneasiness is to seek friendships with people of color. It is certainly good to develop long-term, deep friendships with people from different ethnic cultures, but this does not replace the need to advocate and work for dismantling the systemic racism that affects entire groups of people.

Unfortunately, there is no blueprint offered here. It will take more than individual responses to eradicate racism in this country and repair damaged, broken communities, but individual responses are important. Following are some examples.

Live with the discomfort racism creates. Resist the urge to ignore or reason away the bad feelings that come with realizing that you are privileged and cannot fix the problem alone. While not allowing these feelings to consume you, let them be a spiritual source of motivation to keep active in the fight against racism.

Do not deny the advantages you have, but make a lifetime commitment to end racism. White people don't have to be rich to receive privilege or advantages. You may have grown up poor as a white person. But if you are white and went to public school as a child, chances are that your school received better resources and teachers than the schools in neighborhoods where people of color lived. In addition, you were less likely to be detained, suspended, and expelled for school infractions than people of color were. If you own a home, chances are that you had no problem securing a loan, perhaps even a government loan to get started, and that the value of your property is going up, unlike the value of homes where people of color live. Their neighborhoods are often close to industrial sites and hazardous waste zones. These are generalizations, but if they ring true for you, let them be an added incentive to work to change the system. Consider using more of your resources for this cause.

Listen to what nonwhite groups are saying and demanding. Take advantage of the current public conversation about racism and what people of color suggest as remedies. The Black Lives Matter movement is one popular group that is offering concrete demands. Many public radio and television programs are focusing on what needs to be done to dismantle racism.

Question what you have been taught about other races and are passing on to others, perhaps unconsciously. Otis Moss III explains that prior to the end of the Civil War, Black people were viewed as less than fully human but were not feared for the most part. After the Civil War, a concerted effort was made to teach white people to fear all people of color, especially men, so that they would not compete with white laborers.[12] Today, one needs to watch only a few minutes of the local news to see image after image of mostly people of color getting arrested. This has the effect of maintaining a level of fear of people of color among white people. People of color are engaged in many things that are more positive than robbing others. Many people of color report instances of white people crossing to the other side of the street or clutching their child's hand when a person of color approaches. Challenge assumptions, and think about what you are teaching children about how to interact with people from other backgrounds. They should not be feared any more than white people.

As a Middle Eastern man, Jesus himself likely had dark skin. God is not white either. The Divine is a mystery in whose image all colors of people are made. Challenge places where Jesus and God are portrayed as light-skinned white men, including Sunday school rooms.

Speak up. White people can challenge others when they observe racism. If you regularly observe a security guard following people of color in a store, ask the guard why he or she is only following people of color. If you are afraid of confrontation, report the guard to the manager. If you see police yelling at or roughing up a person of color, make your presence known. If you have a camera, record the situation. It is your right. Some police departments have added body cameras to their officers' uniforms, but until there is a nationwide retraining of police, it is important to have as many eyes as possible on the members of an institution that historically has unjustly harmed people of color.

Show up. When instances of racial violence occur, there are often vigils and protests. The presence of white people is important for showing people of color that it is not *their* problem and that white people are concerned. Showing Up for Racial Justice (SURJ) is a national organization helping organize white people for racial justice. Check out its website (http://www.showingupforracialjustice.org), and see what local groups are participating. Often you can get on a list and be notified when there are events to attend.

Educate yourself. There are no experts on white privilege and racism. It is a lifelong journey, and much more focus is being given to the role white people can play in changing the system. Join or form a reading group to strengthen your actions. Here are some books and articles to consider:

How to Be an Antiracist by Ibram X. Kendi

White Fragility: Why It's So Hard for White People to Talk about Racism by Robin DiAngelo

Dear White Christians: For Those Still Longing for Racial Reconciliation by Jennifer Harvey

The New Jim Crow: Mass Incarceration in the Age of Colorblindness by Michelle Alexander

Slavery by Another Name: The Re-Enslavement of Black Americans from the Civil War to World War II by Douglas A. Blackmon

Yellow: Race in America beyond Black and White by Frank Wu

Blood Done Sign My Name by Timothy Tyson

Privilege, Power, and Difference by Allan Johnson

Privilege: A Reader edited by Michael S. Kimmel and Abby L. Ferber

White Privilege: Essential Readings on the Other Side of Racism by Paul Rothenberg

"Explaining White Privilege to a Broke White Person" by Gina Crosley-Corcoran[13]

Between the World and Me by Ta-Nehisi Coates

The Half Has Never Been Told: Slavery and the Making of American Capitalism by Edward E. Baptist

After the June 17, 2015, massacre of nine Black church members in Charleston, South Carolina, much attention was given to taking down the Confederate flag at the state capitol. In addition, many called not only for taking down some of the statues of white leaders in the capitol who owned slaves and promoted slavery, but also for replacing them with statues of people of color who have contributed to the state's wealth. Look into the white heroes lifted up in your state or city, and find out the history of racism there and what contributions have been made by people of color that have not been given fair recognition.

Is there a museum near you that tells the true story of the genocide of, broken treaties with, and forced relocation of Native Americans; the enslavement of Africans; the Underground Railroad; the internment of Japanese Americans during World War II; or the history of immigrants in your area? Is there a museum nearby that provides information about how part of Mexico was stolen and its citizens became undocumented and unwanted? If so, patronize that museum. Many Jews have funded impressive Holocaust museums around the world. Why are there not more museums in the United States that tell the real story of the effects of racism on people of color?

Attend a White Privilege Conference (https://www.theprivilegeinstitute.com) where you can learn more about white privilege, find out how to combat racism, and network with others.

Give money. Many communities of color in this country suffer from generations of brokenness. Search for groups that are making efforts to transform the people in these communities. For example, give to racial-ethnic colleges or scholarship programs in your area that focus on disadvantaged kids and that help them overcome obstacles.

Conclusion

It is tempting to be overwhelmed and not know where to begin or what to say. The Bible is filled with examples of people who feel inadequate and unqualified to speak. For instance, Jeremiah was a very hesitant prophet, and Jesus' disciples stumbled all over themselves. The Bible also has examples of people with privilege, such as Moses, who stepped up. Moses passed for Egyptian and was safe in Pharaoh's court. But when he witnessed racial injustice, he was compelled to act, despite having no idea of what to say. While white people are not being asked to lead the movement for racial justice, we are in a place where we can challenge unfair advantage and be more active participants in righting the wrongs that harm so many.

CHAPTER 11

THE CHURCH'S RESPONSE

The immediate question when discussing the church's response to racism is, of course, *which* church? Since Jesus assembled the first motley crew of disciples, the community gathered has been anything but a homogenous group of saints. Churches have always been a mixed bag of those who attempt to follow the good news and those who use and twist the message for selfish gain.

European settlers who brought their religion with them to America were no exception. They did not discover anything except a land they had not known existed, filled with people they did not know. Land was mostly stolen, and native inhabitants were forcibly removed. Those displaced did not leave their homes peacefully but resisted. The European settlers—some religious, many not—banded together and formed militias and armies to make room for their "city on a hill," which led to the slaughter of American innocents, the original sin of this country that has yet to be confessed and repaired.

For the most part, church leaders blessed this geno-cide on religious grounds. Leaders would later argue for the inferiority of nonwhite races and justify the enslave-ment of Africans, the criminalization of intermarriage, and the countless invasions of other lands, often distort-ing biblical texts to legitimize their actions and bless injustice.

Not all European Christians in America agreed with the white supremacist system established by the new colonial government. Many white Christians risked their lives to object and protect. But they were the exceptions to the rule. Most Christian churches endorsed racist government policies, which was no surprise, since the government leaders arose from the rank-and-file membership of these same churches.

We also must acknowledge the response of enslaved Africans who were taught biblical stories from their mas-ters and heard words of freedom, justice, and equality. For Otis Moss III, it is no surprise that the Africans rebelled:

> Since we landed on these shores in 1619, and our toes touched the red clay of Georgia and South Car-olina, we have been fighting. Three hundred slave insurrections have been recorded in history, and only three of them did not occur in church. Any time people of color got together and we started worship-ing our God, we knew that our God did not intend for us to be in bondage. We were fighting from the moment that we arrived here.[1]

So today, in a country where even Confederate flag–waving, KKK card–carrying, proud racists identify them-selves as Christian, we need to clarify just which church we are talking about when we discuss the church's response to racism. For our purposes, we are talking mostly about member churches of the National Council of Churches, sometimes called historic or mainline churches. We are talking about churches that, at least for the last quarter of a century, have spoken out in favor of racial justice. Most of these historic, institutional bodies have evolved, participated, and benefited from the racist past and say they want to reckon with it. We will first examine what it means to reconcile and then look at some recent attempts of churches to confront racial injustice.

No Justice, No Reconciliation

Toward the end of his life, Martin Luther King Jr. and other civil rights leaders were increasingly frustrated with the white churches that said they supported the movement for racial justice. When King began his public advocacy work, he was working not for racial integration but for racial justice. Separate but equal was the law of the land, and his efforts were focused not on changing the "separate" part of the law (segregation) but rather the "equal" part. Black bus drivers should be hired to drive in the Black parts of town. If whites could sit in unoccupied Black sections of buses, Black people should be able to sit in unoccupied white sections. King accepted separateness as long as there was equality.

As courageous white Christians and students showed up to support the struggle for justice, however, King was impressed. He soon had a vision of a future beloved community where all would live together in racial harmony. White Christians loved this vision of a beloved community, yet they proved themselves too willing to back away from the ugly fight against racial injustice in order to jump to the kumbaya moment when Christians of all colors would link arms and be one. King insisted that the beloved community could only come about when justice had been done—not before.

Still today, many people of color distrust white-led churches because nothing has been done to fix centuries of racist violence and destruction of communities. Calls and demands for reparations for broken, damaged communities have largely been ignored or downplayed. White-led churches are willing to put energy behind cultural-competency classes so that people can appreciate ethnic differences. We love diverse worship services because they make us look like some beloved community. But people of color ask, "Whose needs are being met? Is this simply meeting the needs of white leaders who are uncomfortable with white privilege and separateness and who want to feel better by sweeping the dirty racial sin under a rug rather than dealing with it?"

Getting to racial reconciliation cannot skip the step of doing justice to communities of color and changing the institutional racism in this country. True reconciliation goes something like this: If a person has been violated, the violator does not get to declare forgiveness and reconciliation before righting the wrong. The role of the violator is to confess what has been done, apologize to the victim, and repair the wrong.

At that point, once justice has been accomplished, it is for the victim to decide whether or not to forgive and whether or not to reconcile with the oppressor. The victim may never wish to reconcile, and the perpetrator must accept that. Sadly, most churches led by white leaders still today want to focus on the beloved community when justice has never been served.

Many white churches concerned about racial justice today feel uncomfortable that Sunday is still the most segregated hour of the week in America. One response is to fix that discomfort by working harder to make people of color feel welcome in white churches. Better yet, white people could join churches led by people of color and learn to follow nonwhite leaders. But perhaps a mostly white church can still do much for racial justice by working with and being led by people of color who may or may not wish to worship with them.

Attempts at Racial Justice

The rest of this chapter offers examples of Christians responding to racial injustice in a variety of ways. Each example is followed by some questions for discussion. Don't let these examples discourage you, but use them to challenge your group to evaluate what you are doing and to urge you onward.

The Black Manifesto

On a Sunday morning in May 1969, James Forman, backed by a large organization of Black leaders, interrupted worship at Riverside Church in New York City and read aloud a manifesto to a startled crowd of worshipers. This document included the following:

> Racist white America has exploited our resources, our minds, our bodies, our labor. . . . We are demanding $500,000,000 from the Christian white churches and the Jewish synagogues. This . . . is not a large sum of money, and we know that the churches and synagogues have a tremendous wealth and its membership, white America, has profited and still exploits Black people. We are also not unaware that the exploitation of colored peoples around the world

is aided and abetted by the white Christian churches and synagogues. . . . Fifteen dollars for every Black brother and sister in the United States is only a beginning of the reparations due us as people who have been exploited and degraded, brutalized, killed and persecuted.[2]

The "Black Manifesto" mentioned using that money to fund a Southern land bank, publishing and printing industries, audiovisual networks, a research skills center, a training center, assistance to the National Welfare Rights Organization, a National Black Labor and Defense Fund, and the establishment of an International Black Appeal to raise money for cooperative businesses in the United States and the African motherland and for a Black university in the South. The leaders of the movement wanted the money in order to help Black communities move forward.

The responses were mixed among the mainline denominations, most of which were visited personally by the group of Black leaders. Not surprisingly, some shut their doors entirely to the group, some defended what they already were doing to help disadvantaged groups of people, and some initiated new programs in response to the manifesto, although they insisted on managing these programs and the funding themselves. Only one denomination gave some money to the Black Economic Development Conference, the organization run by the Black leaders.

Communities of color have made a number of concrete demands for reparations or land returns throughout the centuries. Calls for reparations usually insist on a long-term effort over several generations in order to effect lasting change on the economic and political lives of those affected by racism. They often fall on deaf ears or are rejected immediately by white-led institutions.

> How did your church's leaders respond to the Black Manifesto?
>
> What financial resources does your church give to organizations led by people of color to address needs they have defined?
>
> How would you respond to a modern manifesto by people of color?

Denominational Calls for Racial Justice and Reparations

Since 2000, the Episcopal Church, the Presbyterian Church (U.S.A.), the United Methodist Church, the United Church of Christ, and the Unitarian Universalist Association have all passed resolutions calling for studies of the history of racial injustice, their complicity in it, and the possibility of reparations. Many denominations have created resources to help local congregations engage in study and reflection from their local context. Noteworthy are the United Church of Christ's program "Sacred Conversations to End Racism," which offers resources for local congregations and encourages a host of actions. The Episcopal Church does not have a curriculum, but it does have an antiracism training manual, *Seeing the Face of God in Each Other*, which emphasizes white privilege and the need for justice.[3]

Perhaps the Episcopal Church is the furthest along in terms of calling for confession about slavery on a local and national level. It has passed a number of resolutions on racism and reparations, one in 2006 that urged "the Church at every level to call upon Congress and the American people to support legislation initiating study of and dialogue about the history and legacy of slavery in the United States and the proposals for monetary and non-monetary reparations to the descendants of the victims of slavery."[4] Another resolution passed the same year apologized and repented for the church's participation in slavery and directed every diocese to collect detailed information about how its churches had benefited from slavery.[5] While most churches have not followed through, some impressive accounts have been made by churches built by slave labor. In addition, some public confessions have been made.[6]

The Presbyterian Church (U.S.A.)'s Task Force to Study Reparations delivered a series of recommendations in 2004 that were endorsed by the highest governing body, the General Assembly.[7] One result of this has been the adoption of a new confession by the church, the Belhar Confession, written by the Black Dutch Reformed Mission Church in South Africa during apartheid. Perhaps the PC(USA) still should develop its own national confession about its complicity in racism in the United States.

How has your church benefited from racism? What would have to happen to initiate a conversation about this?

Did the land where your church sits originally belong to others, such as Native Americans or Mexicans? If so, what would racial justice look like?

A Different Approach to Mission

Many Christians have questioned some of the "mission" attempts by people with privilege and power toward groups that would not need help were it not for the injustice caused by the system giving those same missionaries their privilege and power. The relationships built often reinforce the power structure, as help is "given" without questioning the complicity of the giver in a system that produced the need. The shame felt by many churches aware of this dynamic has kept them from engaging in more prophetic, authentic mission, yet others have made justice the center of their mission efforts and used some of their privilege to confront injustice.

In 2002 some U.S. Christians became aware of lethal amounts of lead found in children living in the mining town of La Oroya, Peru. The mine was owned by the Doe Run–Peru Company, a subsidiary of the Renco Corporation of New York. Due to pressure from the United States on Peru's government to lower or eliminate environmental protections in order to do business, the pollution from the metal smelter in La Oroya made the town among the ten worst-polluted places on the planet, and more than 97 percent of its children under age six suffered from lead poisoning. Residents of the town, who needed the jobs, were threatened whenever they complained. Through a partnership with a network of Presbyterian churches and nongovernmental organizations in the United States and Peru called Joining Hands against Hunger, resources were leveraged to document the contamination, create and sustain a media campaign in Peru and the United States, and shame the U.S. company to quit offshoring pollution.[8]

Mission projects of U.S. churches often are inefficient, show an appalling lack of cultural awareness, have a negative effect on local Christian churches or social services, and focus on the personal transformation of U.S. members, often at the expense of local hosts. Yet powerful things can happen when relationships are built on confronting racial and economic injustice.

A number of U.S. churches are turning their mission focus to local efforts around racial justice. For example, some evangelical churches in Eureka, California, raised money to help the Wigot tribe purchase some of its nearby sacred land that had been stolen by the government in the twentieth century and eventually turned into a toxic dump, an all-too-frequent occurrence on Native American lands.[9]

Actions such as this by white churches not only educate white members about racism, but they also give a strong witness to society and government that more must be done to right past wrongs.

The membership of Urban Hope Community Church in Birmingham, Alabama, is over 90 percent Black, and more than 40 percent of its members live below the poverty level. Less than ten minutes away is the mostly white Oak Mountain Presbyterian Church, where 55.7 percent of area homeowners live in homes worth over $300,000. The two churches work together on social projects, including jobs programs and small business support. They have attempted to build relationships that include the white church giving resources but in a way that is not seen as rescuing the poorer church. The pastors, who organized a showing of the movie *Selma* for their congregations to watch and discuss together, say the relationship is not warm and fuzzy but is essential.[10]

Finally, members of Plymouth Congregational Church in Minneapolis are making long-term commitments toward communities of color in their city. After studying the book *The New Jim Crow: Mass Incarceration in the Age of Colorblindness* by Michelle Alexander, they hired a consultant to work with them for two years on white privilege and institutional racism. Their pastor, Theresa Voss, says it is important for a mostly white church to know itself before it can partner with nonwhite churches. The church has constructed a forty-unit housing complex for mentally ill and chemically dependent residents and is now working with other churches to build apartments for seventy-two ex-offenders.

Does your church participate in international mission hands-on projects? If so, who benefits?

Describe how mission projects in your community address racial justice.

Conclusion

In the midst of another period of increased discussion about race relations in the United States, many white churches and leaders have participated in protests against police killings and are making renewed efforts to build bridges with communities of color in their local context. Many other well-intentioned Christians are wondering what to do. Unfortunately, no blueprint exists. But we do know from a painful past that simply focusing on being nice to one another will not change the deep, systemic racism that is firmly rooted in the history of this country. If real change is to happen, it seems obvious that at least two things need to occur in order to take advantage of the moment. First, churches need to focus on doing racial justice and quit declaring some beloved community when justice has not yet been done. Second, a sincere confession needs to be made that includes fixing the wrongs done. That is huge and cannot happen by a single church or institution. But a movement can begin, and perhaps is underway, to work in this direction. Only movement over several generations can undo wrongs and repair damage. Churches, segregated or not, are well positioned to participate in the movement. We have the rich vocabulary and theology of confession, justice, and reconciliation running through the Bible and our tradition. Education is valued by our members. And our hope for God's realm where a beloved community will one day exist inspires us to continue working for justice despite the discomfort and confrontation that happens when we stand up for justice.

Racism was hard-wired into this country from its founding and then through its constitution and religious, social, economic, and political life. Undoing it will take more than reading a book or going to one protest. But change and transformation and hope are also in the DNA of the Christian disciple. Complacency is simply not an option.

NOTES

Foreword

1. Ta-Nehisi Coates, *Between the World and Me* (New York: Spiegel & Grau, 2015), 7.

2. W. E. B. Du Bois, *The Souls of Black Folk* (Mineola, NY: Dover Publications, 1994), 2.

Introduction

1. In the summer of 2015, after nine years at the wonderful Second Presbyterian Church in St. Louis, I moved to Cincinnati to begin an interim pastorate at Mt. Washington Presbyterian Church.

Chapter 1: Defining Terms

1. Joseph Barndt and Charles Ruehle, "Understanding Institutional Racism: Systems That Oppress," in *America's Original Sin: A Study Guide on White Racism*, ed. Bob Hulteen and Jim Wallis (Washington, DC: Sojourners Resource Center, 1992), 12.

2. Barndt and Ruehle, "Understanding Institutional Racism," 14.

3. Tim Jackins, *Working Together to End Racism: Healing from the Damage Caused by Racism* (Seattle: Rational Island Publishers, 2002).

4. Jackins, *Working Together to End Racism*, 1–3.

Chapter 3: The White and Nonwhite Binary, Part 1

1. Howard Zinn, *A People's History of the United States*, twentieth anniversary ed. (New York: HarperCollins, 1999), 8.

2. Quoted in Zinn, *People's History of the United States*, 9.

3. John M. Martin, "Winston Churchill's Cold War: Kissinger Scholar Discusses New Book," *Library of Congress Information Bulletin* 62, no. 1 (January 2003), https://www.loc.gov/loc/lcib/0301/churchill.html.

4. "Strategies for liberation" is a term from Andrea Smith, "Heteropatriarchy and the Three Pillars of White Supremacy," in *Color of Violence: The INCITE! Anthology*, ed. INCITE! Women of Color against Violence (Durham, NC: Duke University Press, 2016), 67.

5. Zinn, *People's History of the United States*, 12.

6. Sydney E. Ahlstrom, *A Religious History of the American People* (New Haven, CT: Yale University Press, 1972), 100.

7. Robette Ann Dias, "Historical Development of Institutional Racism: A Working Paper," revised May 2013, http://www.crossroads antiracism.org/wp-content/themes/crossroads/PDFs/Crossroads%20 Historical%20Development%20of%20Racism.pdf, 28.

8. William Carl Placher, *Readings in the History of Christian Theology: From the Reformation to the Present*, vol. 2 (Philadelphia: Westminster Press, 1988), 107.

9. Zinn, *People's History of the United States*, 12.

10. Frank H. Wu, *Yellow: Race in America beyond Black and White* (New York: Basic Books, 2002), 93.

11. Quoted in Dee Brown, *Bury My Heart at Wounded Knee: An Indian Account of the American West* (New York: Holt, Rinehart & Winston, 1971), 5.

12. Zinn, *People's History of the United States*, 125.

13. John Burnett, "The Navajo Nation's Own Trail of Tears," *All Things Considered*, NPR, June 15, 2005, https://www.npr.org/2005/06/15 /4703136/the-navajo-nation-s-own-trail-of-tears.

14. Ronald Takaki, *A Different Mirror: A History of Multicultural America* (Boston: Little, Brown & Co., 1993), 173.

15. Quoted in Takaki, *Different Mirror*, 174.

16. Takaki, 176.

17. Quoted in Takaki, 176.

18. Michael Simon, dir., *The Axis of Evil Comedy Tour*, DVD (Chatsworth, CA: Image Entertainment, 2007).

19. Steven Salaita, *Anti-Arab Racism in the USA* (Ann Arbor, MI: Pluto Press, 2006), 41.

20. Salaita, 53.

21. "Demographics of Islam," Berkley Center for Religion, Peace, and World Affairs, Georgetown University, https://berkleycenter .georgetown.edu/essays/demographics-of-islam.

22. "Hate Crime Reports Up in Wake of Terrorist Attacks," CNN.com, September 17, 2001, http://edition.cnn.com/2001/US/09/16 /gen.hate.crimes.

23. "Mass LA Muslim Arrests Condemned," BBC News, December 20, 2002, http://news.bbc.co.uk/2/hi/americas/2595391.stm.

24. Abdul Malik Mujahid, "In a Virtual Internment Camp: Muslim Americans since 9/11," Sound Vision, July 2003, https://www .soundvision.com/article/in-a-virtual-internment-camp-muslim -americans-since-911.

25. Maron Bishop and Camilo Vargas, "The Invention of Hispanics," *Latino USA*, May 2, 2014.

26. Aviva Chomsky, *"They Take Our Jobs!" and 20 Other Myths about Immigration* (Boston: Beacon Press, 2007), 167.

Chapter 4: The White and Nonwhite Binary, Part 2

1. Frank H. Wu, *Yellow: Race in America beyond Black and White* (New York: Basic Books, 2002), 94.

2. Quoted in Wu, *Yellow*, 94.

3. Ronald Takaki, *Strangers from a Different Shore: A History of Asian Americans*, rev. ed. (Boston: Little, Brown & Co., 1998), 380–81.

4. Takaki, *Strangers from a Different Shore*, 382.

5. "The US Imprisoned Japanese Peruvians in Texas, Then Said They Entered 'Illegally,'" PRI.org, October 1, 2018, https://www.pri.org /stories/2018-10-01/us-imprisoned-japanese-peruvians-texas-then-said -they-entered-illegally.

6. Gladys Hansen, untitled webpage, Museum of the City of San Francisco, May 1998, http://www.sfmuseum.net/hist9/harvest.html.

7. Gwynn Guilford, "The Dangerous Economics of Racial Resentment during World War II," *Quartz*, February 13, 2018.

8. Kent Rasmussen, *Farewell to Jim Crow: The Rise and Fall of Segregation in America* (New York: Facts on File, 1997), 2.

9. Tom Lewis, *Divided Highways: Building the Interstate Highways, Transforming American Life* (New York: Viking Penguin, 1997), 193.

10. Lewis, *Divided Highways*, 189.

11. David R. Roediger, *Working toward Whiteness: How America's Immigrants Became White — The Strange Journey from Ellis Island to the Suburbs* (New York: Basic Books, 2005), 243.

12. Adam Liptak, "Supreme Court Invalidates Key Part of Voting Rights Act," NYTimes.com, June 25, 2013, https://www.nytimes.com /2013/06/26/us/supreme-court-ruling.html.

13. "Restoring Voting Rights," Brennan Center for Justice, https://www.brennancenter.org/issues/restoring-voting-rights.

14. "2015 Report to the Congress: Impact of the Fair Sentencing Act of 2010," *United States Sentencing Commission*, March 30, 2016, accessed December 13, 2020.

15. "Criminal Disenfranchisement Laws across the United States," Brennan Center for Justice, https://www.brennancenter.org/sites /default/files/publications/images/RTV%20Map.pdf.

Chapter 5: Trumpism

1. Jana Kasperkevic, "What the US Population Will Look Like in 2040," *Business Insider*, March 22, 2012, https://www.businessinsider .com/what-us-population-will-look-like-in-2040-2012-3.

2. Ed Kilgore, "In the Trump Era, Political Incorrectness on the Rise," *New York Intelligencer*, April 9, 2019, https://nymag.com/intelligencer /2019/04/in-the-trump-era-political-incorrectness-on-the-rise.html.

3. Ben Tarnoff, "The Triumph of Trumpism: The New Politics That Is Here to Stay," *The Guardian*, https://www.theguardian.com/us-news /2016/nov/09/us-election-political-movement-trumpism.

4. Olivia Gazis and Stefan Becket, "Senate Intelligence Committee Releases Final Report on 2016 Russian Interference," *CBS News*, August 18, 2020, https://www.cbsnews.com/news/senate-report-russian

-interference-2016-us-election; Rachelle Hampton, "The Most Underplayed Story of the 2016 Election Is Voter Suppression," *New Republic*, October 19, 2017, https://newrepublic.com/minutes/145387 /underplayed-story-2016-election-voter-suppression; Kristen Clarke and Ezra Rosenberg, "Trump Administration Has Voting Rights Act on Life Support," *CNN*, August 6, 2018, https://www.cnn.com/2018/08 /06/opinions/voting-rights-act-anniversary-long-way-to-go-clarke -rosenberg-opinion/index.html.

5. Carol Anderson, *White Rage* (New York: Bloomsbury USA, 2017).

6. Jonathan Metzl, *Dying of Whiteness* (New York: Basic Books, 2019).

7. Stephen Ray, "A Critical Distinction," Facebook, February 18, 2017, https://www.facebook.com/stephen.ray.988/posts/1021090422 9036129.

8. Suzanne Gamboa, "Donald Trump Announces Presidential Bid by Trashing Mexico, Mexicans," *NBC News*, June 16, 2015, https://www.nbcnews.com/news/latino/donald-trump-announces -presidential-bid-trashing-mexico-mexicans-n376521.

9. Jens Manuel Krogstad, "Key Facts about Refugees to the U.S.," Pew Research Center, October 7, 2019, https://www.pewresearch .org/fact-tank/2019/10/07/key-facts-about-refugees-to-the-u-s.

10. Jennifer Wright, "The U.S. Is Tracking Migrant Girls' Periods to Stop Them from Getting Abortions," *Harpers Bazaar*, April 2, 2019, https://www.harpersbazaar.com/culture/politics/a26985261/trump -administration-abortion-period-tracking-migrant-women.

11. Caitlin Dickerson, "Inquiry Ordered into Claims Immigrants Had Unwanted Gynecology Procedures," *New York Times*, September 16, 2020, https://www.nytimes.com/2020/09/16/us/ICE-hysterectomies -whistleblower-georgia.html.

12. Matthew S. Schwartz, "Trump Tells Agencies to End Trainings on 'White Privilege' and 'Critical Race Theory,'" *NPR News*, September 5, 2020, https://www.npr.org/2020/09/05/910053496/trump-tells -agencies-to-end-trainings-on-white-privilege-and-critical-race-theor.

13. Michael Lipka and Gregory A. Smith, "White Evangelical Approval of Trump Slips, but Eight-in-Ten Say They Would Vote for Him," Pew Research Center, July 1, 2020, https://www.pewresearch .org/fact-tank/2020/07/01/white-evangelical-approval-of-trump-slips -but-eight-in-ten-say-they-would-vote-for-him.

14. Robert P. Jones, *White Too Long* (New York: Simon & Schuster, 2020), 161.

15. Maria Godoy, "What Do Coronavirus Racial Disparities Look Like State-by-State?" *NPR News*, May 30, 2020, https://www.npr.org/sections/health-shots/2020/05/30/865413079/what-do-coronavirus-racial-disparities-look-like-state-by-state.

16. Leila Fadel, "Online Memorial Honors Filipino Health Care Workers Who Have Died of COVID-19," *NPR News*, August 1, 2020, https://www.npr.org/2020/08/01/898099601/online-memorial-honors-filipino-health-care-workers-who-have-died-of-covid-19.

17. Cheyenne Haslett and Laura Romero, "Tribes Will Begin to See Some of Coronavirus Relief Money Owed by Federal Government," *ABC News*, May 6, 2020, https://abcnews.go.com/US/tribes-begin-coronavirus-relief-money-owed-federal-government/story?id=70517234.

18. Kelly Anne Smith, "Covid and Race: Households of Color Suffer Most from Pandemic's Financial Consequences Despite Trillions in Aid," *Forbes*, September 17, 2020, https://www.forbes.com/advisor/personal-finance/covid-and-race-households-of-color-suffer-biggest-pandemic-consequences.

19. Haley Willis, Evan Hill, Robin Stein, Christiaan Triebert, Ben Laffin, and Drew Jordan, "New Footage Shows Delayed Medical Response to George Floyd," *New York Times*, August 11, 2020, https://www.nytimes.com/2020/08/11/us/george-floyd-body-cam-full-video.html.

20. Erik Ortiz, "These Confederate Statues Were Removed. But Where Did They Go?" *NBC News*, September 20, 2020, https://www.nbcnews.com/news/us-news/these-confederate-statues-were-removed-where-did-they-go-n1240268.

21. Maura Judkis, "Antiracism Trainers Were Ready for This Moment. Is Everyone Else?" *Washington Post*, July 8, 2020, https://www.washingtonpost.com/lifestyle/style/anti-racism-trainers-were-ready-for-this-moment-is-everyone-else/2020/07/07/df2d39ea-b582-11ea-a510-55bf26485c93_story.html.

22. Philip Bump, "Trump's 2018 Midterm Rebuke Came from the Most Diverse Electorate in History," *Washington Post*, April 23, 2019, https://www.washingtonpost.com/politics/2019/04/23/trumps-midterm-rebuke-came-most-diverse-electorate-history.

Chapter 6: Colonialism, Immigration, and Assimilation

1. On November 25, 1491, the sultan of Granada, Boabdil, signed the Treaty of Granada with Queen Isabel of Castile, Leon, and Sicily, ending the War of Granada and transferring sovereignty of the emirate of Granada to the kingdom of Castile. This treaty marked the end of the 700-year Muslim political presence in the Iberian Peninsula.

2. The Reconquista was the almost 800-year campaign by Iberian Christians to "reconquer" the peninsula from Muslim occupation. It formally ended with the Treaty of Granada in 1491.

3. The Indigenous Values Initiative and the American Indian Law Alliance have curated an educational resource, at https://doctrineofdiscovery.org, with historical, legal, and ecclesial references leading into and repudiating the Doctrine of Discovery. For a historical review and a consideration of the doctrine's implication for congregational work and witness from the Presbyterian Church (U.S.A), see "Doctrine of Discovery: A Review of Its Origins and Implications for Congregations in the PC(USA) and Support for Native American Sovereignty," Report to the 223rd General Assembly, 2018, https://www.presbyterianmission.org/wp-content/uploads/Doctrine-of-Discovery-Report-to-the-223rd-GA-2018-FINALIZED-COPY_As-Approved.pdf.

4. The annexation of Texas is a history imbued with great complexity. The separatist movement that led to the independence of Texas from Mexico was organized by Tejanos—settlers of Mexican origin who predated the U.S. white settlers of the state. The United States' annexation of Texas was mired with the history of slavery. President James Polk manipulated the process of annexation to make sure Texas would join the United States as a state where slave ownership was legal. For more about the U.S. occupation and annexation of former Mexican territory, see *Latino Americans*, episode 1: "Foreigners in Their Own Land," PBS, 2013, http://www.pbs.org/latino-americans.

5. The Mexican-American War (1846–1848) ended with the Treaty of Guadalupe Hidalgo in which the United States formally annexed Texas, New Mexico, and Upper California (modern-day Arizona, California, Colorado, Nevada, New Mexico, Texas, Utah, and parts of Wyoming).

6. The doctrine was attributed to Secretary of State John Quincy Adams but articulated by President James Monroe in 1823. For the text of the doctrine and study resources, see "Monroe Doctrine (1823) and Resource Materials," PBS LearningMedia, https://www .pbslearningmedia.org/resource/a7f270eb-7f2a-4d6c-b9cd -1ac2047742dc/a7f270eb-7f2a-4d6c-b9cd-1ac2047742dc.

7. Fernando Picó, *Vocaciones Caribeñas* (San Juan, Puerto Rico: Ediciones Callejón, 2013).

8. Julie Depenbrock, "Federal Judge Finds Racism behind Arizona Law Banning Ethnic Studies," *All Things Considered*, NPR, August 22, 2017, https://www.npr.org/sections/ed/2017/08/22/545402866/ federal-judge-finds-racism-behind-arizona-law-banning-ethnic -studies; Laura Isensee, "Why Calling Slaves 'Workers' Is More Than an Editing Error," NPR, October 23, 2015, https://www.npr.org /sections/ed/2015/10/23/450826208/why-calling-slaves-workers-is -more-than-an-editing-error.

9. Edouard Glissant, "History-Histories-Stories," in *Caribbean Discourse: Selected Essays* (Charlottesville: University Press of Virginia), 61–96.

10. Michael Weissenstein, "5 Years after Détente with US, Cubans Say Hope Has Dwindled," Associated Press, December 17, 2019, https://www.pbs.org/newshour/world/5-years-after-detente-with-us -cubans-say-hope-has-dwindled.

11. Glissant, "History-Histories-Stories."

12. Ann Crawford Roberts, "A History of United States Policy Towards Haiti," *Modern Latin America*, web supplement for 8th ed., Brown University Library, https://library.brown.edu/create /modernlatinamerica/chapters/chapter-14-the-united-states-and -latin-america/moments-in-u-s-latin-american-relations/a-history-of -united-states-policy-towards-haiti.

13. Peniel Ibe and Kathryn Johnson, "Trump Has Ended Temporary Protected Status for Hundreds of Thousands of Immigrants. Here's What You Need to Know," American Friends Service Committee blog, June 30, 2020, https://www.afsc.org/blogs/news-and-commentary /trump-has-ended-temporary-protected-status-hundreds-thousands -immigrants.

14. Glissant, "History-Histories-Stories."

15. Miguel de la Torre, *Embracing Hopelessness* (Minneapolis: Fortress Press), 134–43.

16. Many argue that because Puerto Ricans are U.S. citizens by virtue of the Jones Act of 1917, they should not be considered immigrants. This argument stems from the metanarrative of Manifest Destiny. It serves the interventionist enterprise of the United States in Latin America and the Caribbean. It also ignores the unique history, culture, and sociopolitical structure of the Puerto Rican identity—one that has very little relation to the dominant U.S. culture and much more in common with Antillean and Latin American histories.

17. Jennifer Hinojosa and Edwin Meléndez, "Puerto Rican Exodus: One Year since Hurricane Maria," Centro (the Center for Puerto Rican Studies), Hunter College, September 2018, https://centropr.hunter .cuny.edu/research/data-center/research-briefs/puerto-rican-exodus -one-year-hurricane-maria.

18. Peace is understood in this case in the sense of the Hebrew term *shalom*. In English, *peace* is often used to refer to the absence of conflict. However, shalom is an articulation of a state of being and a call to action for well-being for the collective.

19. Samuel Silva Gotay, *Protestantismo y Política en Puerto Rico: 1898– 1930* (San Juan, Puerto Rico: Editorial de la Universidad de Puerto Rico, 1997).

Chapter 7: Police Brutality and Black Lives Matter

1. Isabel Wilkerson, "Mike Brown's Shooting and Jim Crow Lynchings Have Too Much in Common: It's Time for America to Own Up," *The Guardian*, August 25, 2014, http://www.theguardian.com /commentisfree/2014/aug/25/mike-brown-shooting-jim-crow -lynchings-in-common.

2. Michelle Alexander, *The New Jim Crow: Mass Incarceration in the Age of Colorblindness* (New York: New Press, 2010), 100.

3. Alan Elsner, *Gates of Injustice: The Crisis in America's Prisons* (Upper Saddle River, NJ: Prentice Hall, 2004), 30.

4. Alexander, *New Jim Crow*, 105.

5. Shannon Sullivan, *Revealing Whiteness: The Unconscious Habits of Racial Privilege* (Bloomington: Indiana University Press, 2006), 40–42.

6. Eric Bradner, "Poll Finds Racial Divide over Wilson Charges," CNN.com, November 24, 2014, http://www.cnn.com/2014/11/24 /politics/ferguson-wilson-cnn-poll.

7. Teresa Welsh, "Views You Can Use: Who Is Listening to Who in Ferguson?" *U.S. News and World Report*, August 18, 2014, http://www.usnews.com/opinion/articles/2014/08/18/race-impacts-perception-of-michael-brown-shooting-death-in-ferguson.

8. Daniel Cox, Juhem Navarro-Rivera, Robert P. Jones, "Race, Religion, and Political Affiliation of Americans' Core Social Networks," Public Religion Research Institute, August 3, 2016, https://www.prri.org/research/poll-race-religion-politics-americans-social-networks/.

Chapter 8: Social Media and the U.S. Racial Divide

1. Zeynep Tufekci, *Twitter and Tear Gas: The Power and Fragility of Networked Protest* (New Haven, CT: Yale University Press, 2017), 3–6.

2. "The Facebook Dilemma: Part One," *Frontline*, PBS, October 29, 2018, https://www.pbs.org/wgbh/frontline/film/facebook-dilemma.

3. Jyothsna Bhat, "Attention Spans in the Age of Technology," National Alliance on Mental Illness blog, August 14, 2017, https://www.nami.org/Blogs/NAMI-Blog/August-2017/Attention-Spans-in-the-Age-of-Technology.

4. Dana Priest, James Jacoby, and Anya Bourg, "Russian Disinformation on Facebook Targeted Ukraine Well before the 2016 U.S. Election," *Frontline*, PBS, October 28, 2018, https://www.pbs.org/wgbh/frontline/article/russian-disinformation-on-facebook-targeted-ukraine-well-before-the-2016-u-s-election.

5. Evgeny Morozov, "From Slactivism to Activism," *Foreign Policy*, September 5, 2009, https://foreignpolicy.com/2009/09/05/from-slacktivism-to-activism.

Chapter 9: Do Segregated Churches Imply Racism?

1. Quoted in Eric Michael Washington, "Most Segregated Hour," March 5, 2015, https://thewitnessbcc.com/most-segregated-hour/.

2. Thomas Jefferson, *Notes on the State of Virginia* (Richmond, VA: J. W. Randolph, 1853), 148–53, http://books.google.com/books?id=DTWttRSMtbYC&printsec=titlepageJefferson. The contention that

Jefferson's book is a blueprint came from A. Smedley and B. D. Smedley, "Race as Biology Is Fiction, Racism as a Social Problem Is Real: Anthropological and Historical Perspectives on the Social Construction of Race," *American Psychologist*, 60, no. 1 (2005): 16–26, https://doi.org/10.1037/0003-066X.60.1.16.

3. James Henretta, "Richard Allen and African-American Identity," in *America's History*, 3rd ed., by James A. Henretta, Elliot Brownlee, David Brody, Susan Ware, and Marilynn Johnson (New York: Worth Publishers, 1997), http://www.earlyamerica.com/review/spring97/allen.html.

4. "Our History," African Methodist Episcopal Church, accessed December 22, 2020, https://www.ame-church.com/our-church/our-history/.

5. Cheryl J. Sanders, *Saints in Exile: The Holiness-Pentecostal Experience in Black Religion and Culture* (New York: Oxford University Press, 1996), 19.

6. Sanders, *Saints in Exile*, 3–4.

7. Charles Reagan Wilson, "Religion and the US South," *Southern Spaces*, March 16, 2004, https://southernspaces.org/2004/religion-and-us-south.

8. LeAna B. Gloor, "From the Melting Pot to the Tossed Salad Metaphor: Why Coercive Assimilation Lacks the Flavors Americans Crave," *Hohonu* 4, no. 1 (2006), https://hilo.hawaii.edu/campuscenter/hohonu/volumes/documents/Vol04x06FromtheMeltingPot.pdf.

Chapter 10: Whiteness and What White People Can Do

1. Jennifer Harvey, *Dear White Christians: For Those Still Longing for Racial Reconciliation* (Grand Rapids: Wm. B. Eerdmans Publishing Co., 2014), 51.

2. Harvey, 48.

3. Harvey, 50.

4. Harvey, 54.

5. Richard Rothstein, Economic Policy Institute research associate, quoted in "Housing Discrimination, Racial Segregation and Poverty in America," *The Diane Rehm Show*, September 16, 2015, https://dianerehm.org/shows/2015-09-16/housing-discrimination-racial-segregation-and-poverty-in-america.

6. Sherrilyn Ifill, president and director-counsel, NAACP Legal Defense and Educational Fund, quoted in "Housing Discrimination, Racial Segregation and Poverty in America."

7. "Overview of 2015 National Urban League Equality Index," State of Black America, http://soba.iamempowered.com/national -equality-index/2015.

8. Thomas Shapiro, *The Hidden Cost of Being Black* (New York: Oxford University Press, 2004), 89.

9. Jose Antonio Vargas, dir., *White People*, MTV documentary, July 22, 2015, https://www.youtube.com/watch?v=_zjj1PmJcRM.

10. Quoted in David Remnick, "Blood at the Root" *New Yorker*, September 28, 2015, http://www.newyorker.com/magazine/2015/09/28 /blood-at-the-root.

11. Robette Ann Dias, "The Black-White Binary Obfuscates and Distorts: Why the Antiracism Movement Must Reject It," *Applying the Analysis* (blog), March 5, 2014, https://applyingtheanalysis.wordpress .com/2014/03/05/the-Black-white-binary-obfuscates-and-distorts-why -the-antiracism-movement-must-reject-it.

12. Otis Moss III, "Hands Up, Black Lives, and Ferguson, Missouri," video, http://empoweringvoicesonline.com/rev-dr-otis-moss -iii-hands-Black-lives-ferguson-missouri (site discontinued).

13. https://medschool.duke.edu/sites/medschool.duke.edu/files/field /attachments/explaining_white_privilege_to_a_broke_white_person.pdf.

Chapter 11: The Church's Response

1. Otis Moss III, *Blue Note Preaching in a Post-Soul World: Finding Hope in an Age of Despair* (Louisville, KY: Westminster John Knox Press, 2015), 100–101.

2. "Black Manifesto," 1969, Archives of the Episcopal Church, https://episcopalarchives.org/church-awakens/exhibits/show/specialgc /black-manifesto.

3. *Seeing the Face of God in Each Other: The Antiracism Training Manual of the Episcopal Church*, 4th ed. (New York: Episcopal Church, 2011), http://www.episcopalchurch.org/library/document/seeing-face-god-each -other-antiracism-training-manual-episcopal-church.

4. Resolution 2006-C011, "Support Legislation for Reparations for

Slavery," Archives of the Episcopal Church, http://www.episcopalarchives
.org/cgi-bin/acts/acts_resolution-complete.pl?resolution=2006-C011.

5. Resolution 2006-A123, "Study Economic Benefits Derived from
Slavery," Archives of the Episcopal Church, http://www.episcopalarchives
.org/cgi-bin/acts/acts_resolution-complete.pl?resolution=2006-A123.

6. See Jennifer Harvey, *Dear White Christians: For Those Still Longing for Racial Reconciliation* (Grand Rapids, MI: Wm. B. Eerdmans
Publishing Co., 2014).

7. "Report of the Task Force on Reparations," Presbyterian
Church (U.S.A.), April 27, 2010, https://www.presbyterianmission.org
/resource/report-task-force-reparations.

8. B. Hunter Farrell, "Form Short-Term Mission to Global Discipleship: A Peruvian Case Study," *Missiology: An International Review*
41, no. 2 (2013): 163–78.

9. Harvey, *Dear White Christians*, 171.

10. Carmen K. Sisson, "Can Churches Lead on Racial Harmony?"
Christian Science Monitor, August 1, 2015, http://www.csmonitor.com
/USA/Society/2015/0801/Can-churches-lead-on-racial-harmony.

ABOUT THE
CONTRIBUTORS

Mary Gene Boteler is the interim pastor at Mt. Washington Presbyterian Church in Cincinnati, Ohio. Before that, she was pastor of Second Presbyterian Church in St. Louis for nine years and was actively involved in the Ferguson protest movement with a remarkable group of interfaith clergy in the area.

Laura M. Cheifetz is assistant dean of admissions, vocation, and stewardship at Vanderbilt Divinity School in Nashville. She contributed to *Streams Run Uphill: Conversations with Young Clergywomen of Color* and *Reflections along the Way*, and she co-edited *Church on Purpose: Reinventing Discipleship, Community, and Justice.*

David Esterline is president and professor of cross-cultural theological education at Pittsburgh Theological Seminary. His teaching and research have focused for several years on ways to respond with courage and faith to the realities of racism and white privilege in the United States.

Jennifer Harvey is professor of religion at Drake University in Des Moines, Iowa. Her books include *Dear White Christians: For Those Still Longing for Racial Reconciliation, Whiteness and Morality: Pursuing Racial Justice through Reparations and Sovereignty,* and *Disrupting White Supremacy from Within.*

Kimberly Jackson is an Episcopal priest in the Diocese of Atlanta. She serves as the Vicar of Church of the Common Ground — a church without walls for people living on the streets of Atlanta. Kim is a founding member of the Atlanta Protest Chaplains. She is also a state senator for the Georgia District 41.

David Maxwell is vice president and executive director for Geneva Press at the Presbyterian Publishing Corporation in Louisville, Kentucky. Throughout his life he has been made aware of his white privilege through various experiences, such as attending the first racially integrated elementary school in Tulsa, Oklahoma, living with undocumented Latin American refugees in New York City, teaching in southern Chile, and living in a bicultural marriage.

Otis Moss III is senior pastor of Trinity United Church of Christ in Chicago. He is ordained in the Progressive National Baptist Convention and the United Church of Christ. His books include *Blue Note Preaching in a Post-Soul World: Finding Hope in an Age of Despair* and *Redemption in a Red Light District: Messages of Hope, Healing, and Empowerment,* and he contributed to *The Gospel Remix: How to Reach the Hip-Hop Generation.*

Debra J. Mumford is the Frank H. Caldwell Professor of Homiletics and associate academic dean at Louisville Presbyterian Theological Seminary in Louisville, Kentucky. A native of Kinston, North Carolina, she earned a

PhD in homiletics and an MA in biblical languages from the Graduate Theological Union in Berkeley, California, and an MDiv from the American Baptist Seminary of the West, also in Berkeley. She also holds a BS in mechanical engineering from Howard University.

Tuhina Verma Rasche is an ordained minister of Word and Sacrament in the Evangelical Lutheran Church in America, serves as the minister of small groups at University African Methodist Episcopal Zion Church in Palo Alto, California, and is the young adult coordinator for Arts|Religion|Culture: A Society for Theopoetics. She has written and spoken extensively on identities within faith spaces and integrating spiritual practices within the self.

Amaury Tañón-Santos is a pastor, a historian, and an intercultural facilitator. His Antillean and Latin American identity as a native Puerto Rican found deep roots in his migration experience to the United States. He pastored congregations in New York and New Jersey and now is on staff at the (Presbyterian) Synod of the Northeast, where he encourages networking, social justice witness, and structural analysis and transformation. His engagement with justice and peace work is also expressed in his passion for urban ministry and organizing and in his commitment to political and theological decolonization.

Jessica Vazquez Torres is a National Program Director at Crossroads Antiracism Organizing and Training. A 1.5-generation ESL Queer Latina of Puerto Rican descent, Jessica has over twenty years' experience in antiracism, anti-oppression, and cultural competency workshop development and facilitation. She has been to seminary twice and enjoys knowing about the creeds, confessions, polity, history, social witness, and social teaching of the religious traditions she works with on their antiracism journey. When not facilitating a conversation, Jessica attempts to become a bread baker, cultivates community with her spouse, Laura, listens to too many books and podcasts at once, walks (sometimes for exercise), and sings songs badly with full abandon.

DeBorah Gilbert White is a diversity, inclusion, and social justice advocate. She is founder and coordinator of HerStory Ensemble, a community organization focused on the social and economic empowerment of women who are experiencing homelessness, who are formerly homeless, and who are at risk of homelessness.

Frank Yamada is executive director of the Association of Theological Schools. He served as the president and Cyrus McCormick Professor of Bible and Culture at McCormick Theological Seminary in Chicago, the first Asian American president of a Presbyterian Church (U.S.A.) seminary. Prior to becoming president, he was the director of the Center for Asian American Ministries and associate professor of Hebrew Bible at McCormick. He is the author of *Configurations of Rape in the Hebrew Bible: A Literary Analysis of Three Rape Narratives* and an editor for and contributor to *The Peoples' Companion to the Bible* and *The Peoples' Bible*, a cross-cultural study Bible.